THE EDUCATION OF
HORSE AND RIDER

THE EDUCATION OF HORSE AND RIDER

A Guide to Basic Dressage
and
Classical Horsemanship for Our Time

JEAN FROISSARD AND LILY POWELL

THE LYONS PRESS
Guilford, Connecticut
An imprint of The Globe Pequot Press

Library of Congress Cataloging-in-Publication Data

Froissard, Jean, 1923–
    [Guide to basic dressage]
    The education of horse and rider : A guide to basic dressage and Classical horsemanship for our time / Jean Froissard and Lily Powell.—1st Lyons Press ed.
        p. cm.
    First work originally published: London : Nelson, 1971. 2nd work originally published: Gaithersburg, Md. : Half Halt Press, c1988.
    ISBN 1-59228-798-0 (trade paper)
    1. Dressage. 2. Horsemanship. I. Froissard, Lily Powell. II. Froissard, Jean, 1923–. Classical horsemanship for our time. III. Title.
SF309.5.F77 2005
798.2'3—dc22
                                                                2005020934

CONTENTS

Foreword	vii
Acknowledgments	viii
Preface	ix
About the Author	xi

PART 1: CLASSICAL HORSEMANSHIP FOR OUR TIME — xiii

Preface to *Classical Horsemanship for Our Time* — xv

Introduction to *Classical Horsemanship for Our Time* — xvii

I.	The Newcomer	1
II.	Early Lunging Lessons	5
III.	Of Bits and Bridles	11
IV.	Aids and the Novice Horse	15
V.	The Grammar of Riding: Balance	21
VI.	Flexions	29
VII.	First Work Under Saddle	47
VIII.	The Neck Rein, When and How	53
IX.	Gymnastics Over Poles	61
X.	The Half-Turns on the Forehand and on the Haunches	65
XI.	Lateral and Longitudinal Suppling	75
XII.	Introduction to the Canter	85
XIII.	The Work on Two Tracks	89
XIV.	Canter, Counter-Canter and Flying Changes of Leg	103
XV.	Pirouettes	111
XVI.	Passage and Piaffe	115

PART 2: A GUIDE TO BASIC DRESSAGE 127

XVII. "To Dress a Horse" 129

XVIII. Riding In Tune 135

XIX. Understanding the Aids 137

XX. The Rider as Trainer and 147
The First Commandment

XXI. The Horse Turns by Both Ends 151

XXII. The Question of Balance 157

XXIII. The Ramener 159

XXIV. The Half-Turn on the Haunches and The Halt 163

XXV. The Rein Back and Rein Aids 169

XXVI. Changing Speeds and Gaits 175

XXVII. The Canter 179

XXVIII. The Second and Third Commandments 185

XXIX. Work on Two Tracks 189

XXX. General Impressions 195

Index 201

FOREWORD
BY GEORGE H. MORRIS

Jean Froissard is not only an old personal friend, but he is also a great horseman, rider, teacher, and trainer. Jean is an intellectual horseman as well as a natural one. He's had the schooling of the very classical French school and understands its principles as few do today.

To rub shoulders with Jean Froissard, either in person, in a clinic, or in print is a lucky moment indeed for any devotee of the sport of the horse. Listen carefully, for he has a lot to say.

GEORGE H. MORRIS
Pittstown, New Jersey, 2005

Jean Froissard (left) with George Morris in the late 1970s.

ACKNOWLEDGMENTS
FOR *CLASSICAL HORSEMANSHIP*
FOR OUR TIME

I am grateful to Lieutenant Colonel Pégliasco, commandant of the cavalry regiment of the Garde Républicaine, to Major Cazelle and to Captain De La Porte du Theil who, each in his own way, made it possible for me to produce most of the photographs illustrating this book. Last, but not least, I am indebted to my two riders, Gratien Cuiburu and Michel Billard, for their devoted patience during our long photo sessions.

PREFACE

Steve Price, loyal friend and editor, suggested a prologue would be useful to introduce the reader to an equestrian education that evolves from the training of a rider facing the initial difficulties of dressage—see A GUIDE TO BASIC DRESSAGE—to that carried on by an experienced horseman able to reach all of its levels up to and including the Grand Prix—see CLASSICAL HORSEMANSHIP FOR OUR TIME.

Except for flying changes at every or second or third stride, canter pirouettes, passage, and piaffe, the paces and movements remain the same throughout, the difference residing in the quality of the performance.

This said, training won't be the same for the future dressage horse, the jumper or the eventer, let alone the hack or trail horse, yet the essentials remain the same.

Along with the natural aptitude that a horse must have for the chosen discipline, its obedience must be complete, whether a jumper or a dressage horse. So must its balance, the keystone of any type of equitation worth the name, as well as straightness. These are the sine qua non that all disciplines share: dressage, jumping, and of course eventing where the horse must combine speed and skill over fences with a respectable showing in the dressage arena.

For a striking example, George Morris and I have given joint clinics in the United States as well as abroad, with the same set of horses and riders doing dressage training on the flat every morning and work over fences every afternoon. Their success has led me to the belief that, at an early stage, the jump rider should perform simple dressage tests just as the dressage rider should in fact exercise over simple fences.

To get back to the core question, in basic training we are looking principally for absence of any hint of resistance; in academic equitation we aim for the greatest possible lightness in perfect balance at all times.

Now, what about the famous precept "calm, forward, straight?" A horse is calm or it isn't, at any level. But the second point is another matter: at an early stage we expect the horse to go forward in response to a reasonably quick action of our legs. At the top level we want to obtain this response at the slightest touch of the boot—upon, to quote the Bard, "a trifle light as air."

In basic training we should perhaps speak of direction rather than of straightness, since all we ask of the horse is not to deviate overall from the straight line he travels on, even if the hind feet do not strictly follow the tracks of the front feet. In academic equitation, however, the hind feet must do so if haunches and shoulders are to move in literal straight-forward synergy.

Let me conclude with a purely semantic note: while in English we now use the word "dressage" exclusively for a certain discipline, it is a borrowing from the French where it simply means "training"—the verb *dresser* means to train. Until a couple of centuries ago, indeed, when English horsemen spoke of dressing, they meant training their horses.

Finally, this reminder: there are no cut-and-dried recipes in equitation. The French have an axiom, "understanding is feeling." What they mean is that what you have not learned to feel you can't truly understand, and without both your message to the horse won't be conveyed. In other words, a means is worth no more or less than how it is conveyed.

JEAN FROISSARD
Paris 2005

About the Author

JEAN FROISSARD is widely recognized as one of the greatest masters of horsemanship. He holds the highest state-conferred degree, that of *Ecuyer Professeur*, a title of the highest distinction within the French Equestrian Federation.

He is the author of the classic works *A Guide to Basic Dressage, Equitation: Learning and Teaching*, and *Jumping: Learning and Teaching*. He and his wife, LILY POWELL, edited the British encyclopedic work *The Horseman's International Book of Reference* and collaborated on works published in France on equestrian social history. They live in Paris.

PART 1:

CLASSICAL HORSEMANSHIP FOR OUR TIME

Complete Horsemanship. Colonel Gustaf Nybleaus, at the time of these photographs (1955) Commander of the Swedish Army Equitation School at Stromsholm, on the horse *Safari:* over fences in the morning, dressage in the afternoon of the same day. All-around horse and horseman

PREFACE
TO *CLASSICAL HORSEMANSHIP*
FOR OUR TIME

In our present world, the number of riders and competitors in the three International Disciplines is constantly increasing. Yet relatively few have the good fortune to possess, or at least have access to, the unique Classical works of bygone days, by such great masters as:

Xenophon: *Hippike* or *On Equitation* (transl. Prof. J. K. Anderson), fourth century B.C.

Antoine de Pluvinel: *Maneige Royal,* 1623, or its heavily edited version produced by a pupil, Menou de Charnizay, *L'Instruction du Roy en exercise de monter à cheval,* 1625.

William Cavendish, marquess, then duke of Newcastle: *Méthode et Invention nouvelle de dresser les chevaux . . . ,* Antwerp 1658 (reprinted in French, John Brindley, London 1737; English translation, id., 1743; C. Corbett, 1748) and *A New Method and Extraordinary Invention to Dress Horses . . . ,* London 1667, this latter one being a different work and published originally in the English language, not translated from the French as was the first.

Gustav Steinbrecht: *Gymnasium des Pferdes,* Berlin 1885.

And last but not least,

François Robichon de La Guérinière: *Ecole de Cavalerie,* Paris 1733; and also *Elémens de Cavalerie,* Paris 1740.

This excellent work, *Classical Horsemanship for Our Time,* by Ecuyer Professeur Jean Froissard is therefore of great help to those riders and competitors who strive for a deeper and more complete insight into the Classical ways of riding, training and developing horses from the lowest to the highest levels. What is more, the author clearly and minutely explains how and why each movement should be executed and improved, be it with young or more experienced horses. No less significant is the author's insistent emphasis on the importance of going slowly, step by step, and rather rewarding the horse for even the smallest improvement than punishing him for the slightest slip. Another important pedagogical advice for times when things go wrong is always to ask oneself: Is it because of some aversion that the horse is unwilling or even resisting, or is it because he does not clearly understand what he is asked to do?

Finally, it is with pleasure that I state how well this work deserves my unreserved recommendation. Let me just suggest that those not well acquainted with the famous French School prepare themselves by an initial look at Chapter IV, "Aids and the Novice Horse," especially at **The Five Rein Effects**.

GUSTAF NYBLAEUS
Former President of the FEI
Dressage Committee

INTRODUCTION
TO *CLASSICAL HORSEMANSHIP*
FOR OUR TIME

The counsel offered by this book, though particularly addressing the dressage rider, should by and large be profitable for horsemen of all disciplines. While only systematic training on the flat can lead to dressage in its genuine sense—that is, near the Prix Saint-Georges and beyond—it is no less fundamental and thus indispensable for upper-level Show Jumping and, obviously, in their more modest expression, dressage and stadium jumping within the framework of Eventing. This fact is more clearly discerned among those of the upscale training and teaching Establishment than among the average horsemen and women whom one meets in the daily exercise of one's profession.

And yet, who would deny that the essence of training, for any purpose, is to render the horse easy to handle and pleasant to ride, where regular paces in and by proper balance ensure his long and trusty service! If basically training is indeed "just that," fundamentally it must be and remain "always that;" even after horse and rider's aptitudes let them accede to the level where, as stated, one can without presuming speak of dressage, that is, the stylization of the natural paces.

Although all horses, if sound, are apt to improve through training, their prospects vary; and it is up to you to make the right choice of your and your work's eventual and sole interpreter in the arena. On your way, remember there are imperatives—general principles—without which the movements performed, no matter how good the "recipes" prescribed, lose all value. One of them is that equitation without impulsion is unthinkable, but that impulsion without calm turns into sheer disorder; another, that rectitude is of the essence, meaning straightness on straight lines, inflexion strictly commensurate with the bend of curved lines, another still, that, be it simple or complicated, the movement must be performed in the proper balance.

It would at all events be foolish to establish a strict progression on paper, immovable in detail, sequence and duration of exercise, and I have not done so. Two words are, in fact, taboo in equitation: *always* and *never*, because they would keep stumbling over exceptions. Even this tenet, I hasten to add, has its exceptions, though they are few, and

---

it is almost "always" to the principles and almost "never" to the means that "always" and "never" may be applied. An absolute truth can be expressed, if you will, in the form of a principle, but only rarely with like rigor in the formulation of a means.

It would doubtless be not only difficult but dangerous to indicate with precision the intensity of hand or leg actions unless in contact with the horse to which these are to be applied, and totally impossible to determine their timing. Anyway, the effectiveness of the aids depends far more on their intelligent use than on the force exerted in the process. Furthermore, hands, legs and seat are but auxiliary to the one aid that is paramount: *that of the mind* which indicates to them when, how and where to intervene. "Action without reflection is but agitation."

I chose to indicate among the proven means those which seem to me least difficult to apply, but more than one road leads to Rome. Beware, nonetheless, of expedients as substitutes to overcome some difficulty or to gain time. No matter how clever, no expedient ever led to a good final result. At first sight they may seem to "turn the trick," but problems will quickly ensue, often more difficult to overcome than those the shortcuts were meant to solve. You will waste time going back to where you can link up again with your original systematic progression, and even more time to erase the wrong lessons from the horse's memory where, regrettably, they tend to cling more tenaciously than the right.

Beware no less of pseudo-scientific theories. While doubtless science has a part in equitation, its contribution is quite modest to a pursuit which is and should remain an art. Is a painter's genius in using color based on his acquaintance with chemistry, or a pianist's brilliance on his knowledge of physics and the number of vibrations emitted by the notes drawn from his instrument? The truth we face applies even more forcefully to equitation where we are working with a living being, by definition changing and whose reactions are hardly ever quite identical to identical actions, even if the rider were able to realize the unrealizable: to repeat the same action with exactly the same intensity of aids in exactly the same position, and this at the fleeting moment when the horse's legs are again in the same position and his weight, in the same balance, distributed on them in the same way.

Ride your horse as you feel him, provided you were born to, or over the years have learned to feel! It is the one thing no book can teach, no teacher give you, the one conquest the laurels of which will be entirely yours.

I.
THE NEWCOMER

What, you might ask, is the ideal horse to buy? Let me say from the outset that, no matter how much you can afford to invest, the ideal horse does not exist. This said, you should be able to distinguish between acceptable and disqualifying faults. Your choice will moreover depend on the use you intend to make of your mount. Make up your mind, *then only* pick the suitable type. While all true riding horse breeds are apt to serve, the individual to choose must be trainable up to the single flying change of leg and have a little jump in him. He must be a willing performer, neither excitable nor lethargic. Since, above all, he must be sound, **you must have him vetted** (by a vet of your own, not the seller's) to be sure he is sound inside and out because "a horse does not travel on his legs alone, but on his heart, his lungs, his digestive tract, and his nerves." Only a veterinarian can check all this and his eyes. What *you* must learn to judge as a horseman or woman is conformation, that is, *bodily harmony*. What good is a splendid forehand with weak quarters, or the reverse?

A checklist followed by my students will help you as a starter.

- ☐ Is he built in a slightly ascending line with a clearly defined withers extending well back?
- ☐ Is his back short, broad and very muscular?
- ☐ Are his loins short, broad, straight and well muscled?
- ☐ Is his croup long, muscular and slightly sloping?
- ☐ Is his chest deep and wide?
- ☐ Is his neck of medium length, standing out well, with a slant 45° above the horizontal, neither too thick nor too thin?
- ☐ Is his head square, lean, expressive and well set on? It is a sign of quality, shun the heavy head.
- ☐ Is his shoulder long and sloping?
- ☐ Is his arm long, muscular and rather straight?
- ☐ Is his breast muscular and rather wide?
- ☐ Is his forearm long, vertical and strong, with prominent muscles?
- ☐ Is the direction of the elbow right? If it is glued to the body, the horse will be splay-footed; if excessively spread, he will be pigeon-toed.

☐ Are the cannons short, dense and lean?

☐ Are the fetlocks broad and neat?

☐ What about the length and direction of the pasterns? They should be quite, but not exceedingly, long and sloping.

☐ Are the thighs long, almost vertical, powerfully muscled?

☐ Are the gaskins long, broad and muscular?

☐ Are the hocks lean, neat, wide open?

☐ Are cannons, fetlocks and pasterns equally good in all respects on fore and hind legs?

☐ Are the feet sound and the legs normal in their formation?

The horse should, above all, be examined in action where he must be energetic without excitation. The tail carried aloft is an indication of vigor. The paces should be easy and fluent on both hands, the set of the legs as normal in action as they were at the halt.

Stay away from the often clunky "warmblood" and do not even think of such eccentric crossbreeds as Thoroughbred and Percheron where the draft horse dilutes what the bloodhorse pours in. Whatever fabulous performance by such a riding-*cum*-draft-horse mixture someone may cite, it is but the very rare exception to a hard and fast rule. Another rule (felt by many riders to be so hard indeed that they continually infringe upon it) is that *below the age of four a horse is too young to go to school!*

Mutual Expectations

Training in its very earliest stage means teaching the horse understanding of the rider's language; you are the teacher, which presupposes that you speak this language exceedingly well. But you must also know and understand your pupil's idiom; for conversation, let alone agreement, cannot exist where one partner speaks without trying to hear while the other is expected to listen without being heard. Are you, then, sufficiently bilingual to teach your horse a second language? If indeed so, "the dumb animal" will be surprisingly quick to learn.

Start with simple statements, clearly enunciated and full of common sense, the only language a horse will understand. What is common sense chiefly based on, particularly with an adopted youngster, be he child or colt? On observation first of all: observation of your horses's behavior at rest, at play and at work under saddle when you can feel, and at liberty when you can see him. For the characters of horses, like those of humans, are of infinite variety. Again, *you* are the teacher and therefore it is up to *you* to understand *him*, not up to *him* to understand *you*. Remember, too, that he who wishes to receive must know how to give, not only of his heart but of his mind.

Keep in mind that at this point we are still concerned with training in its earliest meaning, when he as yet knows little of man and nothing of the horseman. While at a much later date it may or may not turn into an art, its essential purpose is, then as now, to give him good manners and ability through the development of his physical and mental qualities in order to make him easy to use and pleasant to ride.

Most of us know that in its original innocence *(also in English throughout the eighteenth century)* the catchword *dressage*, which so torments many an ambitious rider, had the simple meaning of Webster's correct definition:

"Dressage (F. preparation, straightening, training, fr. *dresser*, to prepare, make straight, train - age - more at DRESS): the execution by a horse of a set of maneuvers without such perceptible aids as voice and reins . . . , also the systematic training of a horse in obedience and deportment."

Yes, essentially you prepare your horse and make him straight for that "dressage test" which will evaluate what your "dressage" (i.e., training) has accomplished. To complete the picture, let us recall Gen. L'Hotte's definitive statement on the matter, **Calm, Forward, Straight,*** which, save for some overlapping, gives us in fact the chronological order of our training progression.

If the very first step is to win your novice horse's trust, this confidence gained in the beginning must be jealously preserved from first to last and at every step along the road. But this can only be done by someone competent enough to have a definite sense of his pupil's capabilities—never to be exceeded—and who will apply the training principles in a sequence logical yet flexible enough to adjust to the particular horse by close attention to his reactions; never impatient, yet without falling into the sort of pseudo-patience that rather more resembles resignation, which gives in and then gives up.

Upon arrival and for about three weeks, isolate your proud, but as yet unknown, acquisition from your other horses, if any, to prevent the

---

*General Alexis L'Hotte, *Questions Equestres*, Paris, 1906, the seminal turn of the century work recognized to have laid the philosophical foundation of modern horsemanship. The quotation *calme, en avant, droit* from the book has turned into the fundamental equestrian motto in every language.

spread of something he might be "bringing in." On the morning following, exercise him inside the riding hall or, if not lucky enough to have one, make for some enclosed space. In the end, you can retrieve him easily if you keep him in a halter and court him with a carrot rather than sugar; for many horses sugar is but an acquired taste.

Do not start "working" him for a week or so to come; turn him out if you have a paddock. Whenever possible, spend time with and speak to him, not just to win his heart but because, once training begins, your voice will be your most precious aid by which to accompany and thereby convey the meaning of all physical requests. For the time being, at any rate, you have no other means of association, just the caress of the voice which gentles and reassures and the carrot or handful of oats offered with the word "come." Do not stand farther than three feet away from him, sometimes closer; until he has learned to appreciate your offerings he should be spared the stress of fetching them. And before he does respond to "come," don't even think of putting him to work. So that he may associate his greatest pleasures with your presence, feed him at mealtimes by your own hand; it will help you immeasurably in his later training.

The choice of a stablemate is of great importance. Congenial company at rest is a relaxant, animosity an irritant, to humans and animals alike. When the farrier arrives for a first, *light* shoeing, stay with your charge as you would with your child at the doctor's office, and keep doing so until shoeing becomes a familiar experience. Carefully watch his feed and droppings. If all is normal for a week or so, you may begin to work him lightly, careful not to overtax him. **Do you know what is enough and what too much?**

Apollo exhorted the ancients with the words, "Nothing to excess," yet also added, "know thyself."

II.
Early Lunging Lessons

Lunging work seems to be the stepchild of the riding community, though it constitutes quite possibly the most decisive "childhood impression" for a horse's entire future. Far from a waste of time, moreover, these lessons will greatly facilitate your subsequent work.

I will therefore discuss at some length lunging as practiced at this early stage. Later, geared to other purposes, it may assume the character of an art. The sight of an extremely gifted horseman lungeline in hand becomes an almost aesthetic pleasure. Even in the case in question, lunging if well done is far from easy.

Your present purpose is to habituate the horse to your voice, to teach him to obey it, and this in time without recourse to lungeline or lunging whip. Until such a day, however, the two remain your "interpreters" and while much depends on your skill in their handling, a great deal also will depend on your skillful choice.

For perfect adjustment of the cavesson, its noseband carries jointed *well padded* metal pieces on either side. These are to the cavesson what the tree is to the saddle; without them the gear has no advantage over a simple halter. At this stage, we prefer the cavesson to the snaffle because its action is more natural and stronger, yet spares the mouth.

For maximum effect without harming parts of the head, it must be as well adjusted as any bridle. It should rest on the base of the nose but not so low as to interfere with breathing. Tighten the noseband sufficiently to keep it from turning and perhaps letting one cheekpiece hurt the eye. Leave the throatlatch loose enough for comfortable respiration. To steady the cheekpieces, some cavessons carry a second strap which, like the throatlatch, passes from cheekpiece to cheekpiece underneath the lower jaw, between the throatlatch and the cavesson itself.

The heavier the lungeline, the stronger is its action on the cavesson which, in turn, exerts a stronger action on the horse. Far better to have a lighter one, very supple and quite wide (a good inch or so), a light snaphook buckling it to the central cavesson ring. Some end in a chain about two feet long; do not use them. Details these may be, but important ones if the horse is to stay on the circle and the line is to remain taut. Fold it in a figure eight pattern rather than twist it round your hand where a horse's sudden pull can saw or crush your fingers.

For proper balance in hand, choose a lunging whip with a rather heavy pommel, 15 feet in length divided just about evenly between grip and thong. And while at the tackshop, get your horse boots against possible injury to his cannons.

But how to use the lungeline? By oscillations: horizontal when to put distance between you and your horse; vertical (making the cavesson act vertically on his nose) for a slowdown and all the way to the halt, depending on vigor, repetition and the extent of the horse's obedience.

The elementary work we are here dealing with remains unchanged whether training a young or an adult horse; only the time factor varies, and this is determined by the results achieved. Remember that the chief result you seek is to have him *literally listen* to you. Everyone gives lipservice to the voice as an aid, but few make use of it. Yet it is precious in early training. More important, I daresay, than either hands or legs whose meaning only your voice can explain to the horse. It becomes in fact superfluous, hence useless only by the time submission no longer leaves anything to be desired; that is, when the horse is trained! For obedience, as for all other aspects of training, there are different consecutive levels on the way to the dressage arena where the voice aid is logically banned, since the horse is supposed to understand and perform what the test demands. Outside of this particular and rather less than everyday occurrence, the voice must be looked upon as a normal aid to be used as often as required.

The shadings of the voice are almost always instantly understood by the horse, which is far from true for legs and hands. The *shadings*, mind you, for people tend to forget that, while the horse has a highly developed acuity of hearing and though he understands the voice, it is the music of the song he reacts to, not the words. How often do I hear the word "trot" ring out in the very same tones as "canter." Your voice can also grant reward or mete out punishment, can calm or incite, provided you speak "horse language." Voice punishment indeed has often a stronger, I would say deeper, effect than a whiplash, and this without the attendant upset. "The action of the voice," said Fillis, "has frequently been of great help to me, getting me out of many a difficult spot." The voice contrary to legs and hands, not being of just local action, affects the horse in his entirety. So do not skip these lessons, teach your youngster obedience to the orders of your voice until he walks, trots, canters and halts without leaving the circle.

Boots on his legs, cavesson adjusted, lunging whip in hand, lead him into the school or smallish fenced-in outdoor space. If you place yourself in a corner, it will frame your circle (about 15 feet in radius) on two sides. Before making any demands on him, let him kick up his heels a bit; freshly out of the stables, full of life and totally untrained, he would otherwise almost surely disobey you, only to find out that he can get away with it. So let him carry on for a while, content to let your voice do the soothing. The whip is almost useless at this point in time; until he gets to know it better, hold it like an ordinary whip, pommel between thumb and index finger, the tip (lest you frighten your ignorant friend) behind you. A simple rotation of the wrist will ready it for use. Needless to say that on a left-hand circle the lungeline is held in the left hand, the whip in the right. Watch out, though, when you send him onto the circle or when, having walked beside him, you return to your place: moving alongside the lungeline, head turned outside, quarters inside, he may lash out with his hindlegs. So keep the lungeline taut enough to draw his head inward where it opposes the haunches.

After five minutes or so, ask for an *active* trot on that 15 foot circle. Three things may now happen: he either keeps trotting, which is fine, so let him continue; or he slows down or falls into a walk, when you must gently nudge him on with the whip pointing downward *behind* his quarters, your voice telling him, "trot." Or else he breaks into a canter which you let him do for a few seconds, telling him, "tro-o-o-t," in softer, drawling tones. This usually suffices but, should he persist, a few vertical oscillations of the lungeline will bring him back down to the trot.

As to maintaining the horse on the circle, do not just yet ask for too much. If he tries to come to the center, reinforce the horizontal oscillations, if necessary, by now pointing the lunging whip in the direction of the shoulder. If, on the contrary, he tries to shift outside, your circle may be just a bit too small, so let the lungeline slip a little. If this won't do, remember that one fourth of the circle is nicely framed by the walls; so during passage through the corner you only need minimum lungeline tension, but during the remaining three-fourths draw his head to the inside by brief little jerks. Beware, however, of pulling on him by hanging onto the line. He will eventually understand that the cavesson only acts when he pulls, by those brief, repetitive and disagreeable tractions which he will logically decide to avoid.

Soon the time will have come for a bit of rest. If "at a wa-a-alk" is not sufficient, a few vertical oscillations accompany your voice. If this remains unheeded, ask for a halt, "oh-ho," along with a good shake on the cavesson, as he enters the corner and while you move parallel to him toward one of the walls. With his nose against this piece of wall, framed on the outside by the other one and on the inside by you and the lunging whip, he will stop. This is indeed the proper fashion to ask for the very first halts, combining voice and lungeline, against the wall, the fastest way to his understanding.

If problems arise in your work at the walk, take hold of the lungeline close to the cavesson and walk alongside him, asking for frequent brief halts, ever associating voice and cavesson action in halting, voice and lunging whip in walking on. By and by, step away from him until, very gradually, you once more reach the center of the circle.

Forget departures at the canter until your pupil is better acquainted with the work at walk and trot, calm and truly cognizant of the meaning of your orders. At that time you may go on to work at the canter, proceeding just as you did before. Here patience is particularly important because the horse must start into the canter without speeding up the trot. Ideally, in fact, the departures should be prompted from the walk, though for now quite an impossible proposition. On the other hand, make sure he strikes off well; you do not want him to learn to depart through *loss* of balance when under saddle he will be expected to do so by *assuming* a given balance.

Novices tend to position themselves wrongly in relation to the horse. Stand at the center, lunging line and whip forming the two sides of a V, thus framing the horse, although this position will in the course of the work vary a bit as needed. If, for example, you want your horse to slow down, you approach his shoulder; the haunches, if you need to drive him on. Whichever, keep a taut line.

In lunging, as under saddle, your lessons should not be long. Half an hour is plenty, at first fifteen to twenty minutes are enough. Needless to say, the work is done on both reins, a little more on the more difficult one. Better a second brief lesson in a day than a single long one.

Just as naturally, you won't miss an opportunity to reward your horse with cherishings or tidbits and, in doing so, walk up to him rather than draw him toward yourself. This will teach him from the very start respect for both immobility and the circle. Only later may he be taught to come to the center and, subsequently, to change rein, exercises without discernible use for training proper. They serve but a specific purpose and, unless very well done, are liable to confuse the horse. The essential is to get him to stand perfectly still, since immobility is the key to your progression.

Also, without fearing, much less spooking at its sight, he must become thoroughly familiar with and respectful of the lunging whip as an aid. After a dozen lessons of this regimen, there should be considerable progress in submissiveness, calm and trust. So, after a lesson where (having been asked for little and made much of at the giving) he has shown himself particularly trusting and calm, you will step up and hold the lungeline twenty inches from the cavesson ring. You slide the lunging whip (grip and thong in your right hand) in a caressing gesture along his back, speaking to him all the while in a reassuring tone of voice. In time you will be able to do so with the thong alone.

While a mere ten days ought to suffice to accustom the horse to being attentive and trusting in this elementary work, beware of smugness. The result must be firmed up through perservering daily work and as much repetition as necessary without it turning into mere routine. For you must know how to "animate" these lessons by diversified work, frequent letups, and moments for patting, or you will dull and blunt your horse's mind.

Within three to six weeks you should have achieved quite a bit:

From a physical standpoint, this time span corresponds to that required for acclimatization and adaptation to unaccustomed feed. It also allows for light muscle-building work without the encumbrance of your weight on a young back.

As concerns the training angle, it is sufficient to win his confidence, while laying the foundations of your authority by lunging line and whip and making him understand and obey the various intonations of your voice.

Although gradually shortened, these lessons on the lungeline should continue throughout the entire first year.

III.
OF BITS AND BRIDLES

We bit the "new" horse with a snaffle, and there is none better for this purpose than the Baucher snaffle. Whether single or double jointed, it remains straight in the mouth, all others coming at their center to rest on the tongue. Since, moreover, it possesses upper cheeks to which the cheekpieces are buckled, it is not liable to slip, or pinch the corners of the mouth. The Y-mouth snaffle, on the other hand, is useful if your horse is a bit too frisky, and its dual mouthpiece is more relaxing than the single ones. That, unlike the Baucher snaffle, it is not admitted in dressage tests is of no present concern to us.

When comes the time to replace the snaffle with a full bridle? This depends not only on the horse but on his trainer's capacities. One thing to remember is that if a horse goes well in a simple snaffle, he will go as well in a full bridle, while the reverse is not always true. And by the time you use the full bridle, you will do well to return intermittently to the simple snaffle, thus confirming that the horse has lost none of his lightness to the hand.

Correct adjustment of the full bridle is of the essence if you want to reap all the benefits it has to offer and guard against otherwise inevitable problems. Most horses go well in a half-moon curb bit, the simplest and gentlest of all. If the horse's tongue is thick to the point of being squeezed by this bit, you may want to pick a port-mouth bit. Whatever you may choose, shun the sliding mouthpiece, because (a) it causes the hand on the reins to lose its precision at the moment of action on the bars and (b) it incites the horse to turn into a "blabbermouth," never ceasing to chew on it from the moment he is bridled.

The width of the curb bit must coincide with that of the mouth, with less than 1/16 of an inch in excess on each side. The upper cheeks must swivel easily under tightening reins; if the width of the upper jaw impedes this, a bit with its upper cheeks farther apart than the lower ones will solve the problem.

The curb bit must be first fitted to your horse's mouth, its place determining that of the snaffle. Its mouthpiece must act on the bars and the bridoon is placed slightly above, even at the risk of somewhat puckering the corners of the mouth. The curb chain must rest perfectly flat below the curb groove with which it is to come in contact when the lower cheeks of the curb are tilted at a 45 degree angle under the action of the reins. The addition of a lipstrap will keep the horse's teeth from worrying the lower cheeks of the bit. If you decide to use a drop noseband, remember prior to adjustment that it is frequently in fighting the discomfort of its excessive tightness that horses learn to open their mouths.

Finally, such gears as standing martingales or running reins are out of place in the training of a dressage horse for two reasons, either one of which would suffice to discard them. One, if the horse poses such management problems, you picked the wrong horse. Secondly, a gear will obtain nothing that the hand could not. If on rare occasions a certain result can be reached more quickly, their use is more difficult than that of your own God-given hands.

Fig. 1. Snaffle and curb bits

Snaffle, Pelham and curb bits

1 Fillis bridoon; 2 Australian loose ring cheek snaffle; 3 Baucher snaffle; 4 Y-mouth snaffle; 5 Eggbutt German mouth snaffle; 6 Dee cheek twisted race snaffle; 7 Balding gag; 8 Hartwell Pelham; 9 Angle cheek Pelham; 10 Jointed Pelham; 11 Kimblewick; 12 Fixed cheek arch mouth curb; 13 Slide cheek Weymouth with port

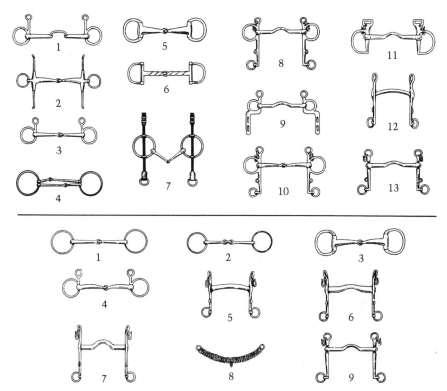

Bridoons and curb bits authorized by the FEI

1 Ordinary bridoon; 2 French bridoon; 3 Bridoon with eggbutt ring; 4 Baucher bridoon; 5 Fixed cheek arch mouth curb; 6 Curb bit with incurved upper cheeks; 7 Curb bit with port; 8 Curb chain; 9 Slide cheek Weymouth bit

Fig. 2. Bridles, cavesson and nosebands

The parts of the bridle

1 Noseband; 2 Headstrap; 3 Headpiece; 4 Throatlatch; 5 Cheekpieces; 6 Bridoon sliphead; 7 Bridoon cheekpiece; 8 Browband; 9 Pelham roundings; 10 Curb chain with fly link for lip strap; 11 Lip strap; 12 Snaffle or bridoon reins; 13 Curb reins

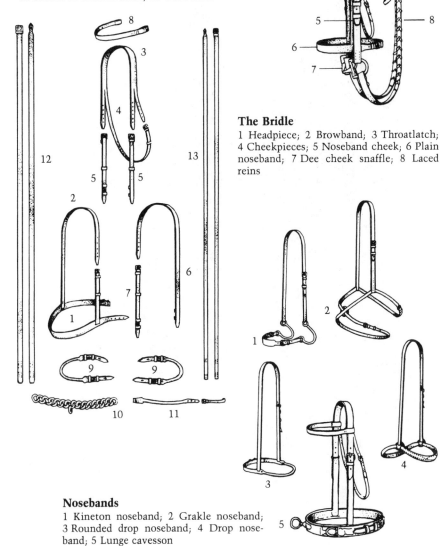

The Bridle

1 Headpiece; 2 Browband; 3 Throatlatch; 4 Cheekpieces; 5 Noseband cheek; 6 Plain noseband; 7 Dee cheek snaffle; 8 Laced reins

Nosebands

1 Kineton noseband; 2 Grakle noseband; 3 Rounded drop noseband; 4 Drop noseband; 5 Lunge cavesson

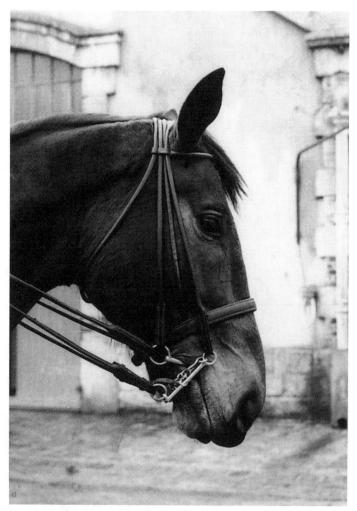

Fig. 3. The Well-Adjusted Bridle. The cheeks of the curb bit form a 45 degree angle when reins and curb chain are stretched.

IV.
AIDS AND THE NOVICE HORSE

Few of the natural or artificial aids have meaning for a horse in early training and yet, from this sparse base we must build up a simple common language. Under favorable conditions, though, this idiom may become extremely varied, subtle and discreet. Such eventful fine-shading of the aids is arrived at by a process of substitutions, as when for instance we pass from the use of the lunging whip to that of riding whip and voice to teach the horse the meaning of the propulsive action of the legs. The legs, in turn, will subsequently be applied in different ways, to different places, and in different degrees of intensity.

No aid, however, is effective unless precise and precision in turn depends on steadiness which depends on a firm seat. From an unsteady rider the language of the aids only emanates as a splutter or an incoherent stammer. Thus one may say that the education of the taught reflects the education of the teacher.

Remember a truism so blatant one neglects to keep it in mind: a horse cannot obey a gesture unless aware of its sense and prepared and fit to carry out the order conveyed. Yet, unless the horse has repeatedly carried out the same command imparted by the very same aids, a rider cannot ever be quite certain of having been understood. Thus in equitation obedience is the only warranty of comprehension.

While one can recommend a given aid for a given movement, may even explain the technical whys and hows, the rider's feel for measure and timing will make the difference between fumble or ease. Feeling is to the rider as the ear to the musician: it can be developed but not acquired where the predisposition does not exist.

The names of the several categories of aids—natural and artificial, upper and lower, lateral and diagonal, active and supporting—are self-explanatory but it may be useful to remind ourselves that the hands and legs can

Act, Yield or Resist.

The hands act when they increase rein tension for a slowdown, a halt or a rein back; for a change of head or neck carriage, or of direction; for a half-halt* or a vibratory effect.

---

*Half-Halt—"A firm upward gesture on taut reins, followed quasi instantly by a gradual relaxation of initially tightly closed fingers and a yielding of the hand. This action may be compared to the successive gestures made when lifting a heavy stone off the ground at the foot of a staircase, then placing it on a higher step, yet without causing the slightest damage or noise." *Academic Equitation* by Gen. Decarpentry.

They *yield* when their relaxing fingers diminish rein tension in a range from mere softening of touch to complete relaxation.

They *resist* when opposing an initiative taken by the horse, opposing in fact the pull of any sort of force, whether from the horse's mouth or the rider's own wrist, although steadying the hand does not automatically imply immobility of fingers.

The legs *act* in order to prompt movement; to maintain or increase speed; to augment engagement; to obtain either a lateral mobilization of the haunches or a bend.

They *yield* when, interrupting all action, they slacken and drop by their own weight in only light contact with the horse's flanks.

They *resist* when opposing a lateral shift, if caused by the horse's own initiative.

In training, notably in the early stages, discretion of the aids is definitely secondary to their clarity, since our immediate concern is to make ourselves understood. One does not ride a colt as one does in the dressage arena. Initially ample movements will be decreased gradually to a point of discretion where the hands appear all but motionless. A hand called "steady" is said so in relation to the horse's mouth, not the pommel, and once the horse's neck and head have become steady, a mere opening or closing of the fingers will in most cases quite suffice.

But the effectiveness of hand action depends largely on the relaxation of shoulders, elbows, wrists and fingers. Stiffness of elbows—and therewith arms and forearms from shoulders to wrists—will affect the smallest gesture of the fingers. The horse, which feels this stiffness in its mouth, will react in one negative way or another, depending on its character and sensitivity, while nine times out of ten it would yield to an action equally strong but smooth. Of all fingers, only thumb and index must remain firmly locked to keep the reins from becoming uneven while the rest are allowed full play, a thing admittedly easier to understand than do.

Speed is controlled by fingers closing over the reins, wrists raised vertically and turned briskly outward (a "turn of the key"), the body weight being brought to bear on the ends of the reins, but do beware of traction; rather oppose to the horse, as explained, a *wall* extending from shoulders to fingers.

Direction is changed by five different rein effects, as follows:

The Five Rein Effects

The opening rein (1st effect) has a natural action upon the horse. It consists of drawing his nose in the direction one wants to take. To turn right, make your right wrist pivot a quarter right turn, thereby turning your nails up, and shift it to the right, keeping your elbows close to the body.

The counter-rein (2nd effect) also called, the neck rein, acts upon the base of the neck which it nudges in the proposed direction. To turn right, make your left wrist act from left to right and from back to front. It is the only rein effect permitting you to manage your horse with a single hand. Unlike the opening rein, the horse, able to evade it without trouble, must be trained to obey it.

Both rein effects act on the forehand which takes the new direction, while the hindquarters are content to follow the shoulders in this change. Since the action does not interfere with the forward movement, the horse does not tend to slow down.

By contrast the following three rein effects address the hindquarters. By a rational disposition of his reins, the rider opposes the shoulders to the haunches, whence their appellation of reins of opposition. This opposition impairs the forward movement which the rider's legs must painstakingly keep intact or restore whenever it tends to disappear; and the effectiveness of these reins is commensurate with the degree of activity the rider creates in the hindquarters.

The right direct rein of opposition (3rd effect) acts upon the haunches and makes the horse turn right by pushing his haunches to the left. In performing this rein effect, the rider tightens the right rein in the direction of his right knee, after slightly relaxing the fingers of his left hand so as to make the horse understand more easily the action of the right. With this effect the reins remain parallel to the horse's axis.

The right counter-rein of opposition in front of the withers (4th effect) acts upon the shoulders and makes the horse turn left by throwing his shoulders to the left and his haunches to the right; the horse thus pivots around an axis passing approximately through the vertical of the stirrup leathers. In performing this rein effect, the rider, increasing finger pressure on the right rein, shifts his right wrist to the left, passing in front of the withers.

The right counter-rein of opposition passing behind the withers (5th effect or intermediate rein) acts upon the shoulders and the haunches and displaces the whole horse toward the left. This rein effect is intermediate between the direct rein of opposition, which only acts upon the haunches, and the counter-rein of opposition in front of the withers, which only acts upon the shoulders. It thus falls to the rider, in shifting his right wrist toward the left, to determine how far behind the withers the right rein should pass in order to act with equal intensity upon shoulders and haunches. The more this intermediate rein tends to approach the direct rein of opposition, the more it acts upon the hindquarters and, on the contrary, the more it tends to approach the counter-rein of opposition in front of the withers, the greater its effect on the forehand.

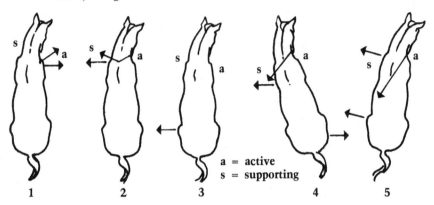

a = active
s = supporting

Fig. 4. The Five Rein Effects. (1) The opening rein; (2) The counter-rein; (3) The direct rein of opposition; (4) The right counter rein of opposition in front of the withers; (5) The right counter-rein of opposition passing behind the withers.

Remember, however, that

(a) the number of these rein effects is but a basic one to be broken down and combined into a myriad shades, depending on the rider's tact and the horse's level of training, and that the shifting of the hands, ample with the colt, must become merely incipient with the trained horse;

(b) the effectiveness of any of the five is contingent on that of the legs, hand action without impulsion coming virtually to naught;

(c) the role of the supporting hand is almost more decisive than that of the acting one.

Now, on paper it is easy to separate the action which slows down from that which changes direction. During exercises we can still without any problem practice pace variations only, or only changes of direction. But in actual riding it is a different story, for the hands are often called upon to accomplish several tasks at once: to request a slowdown, for example, during a change of direction and perhaps during this change to straighten a horse which leans to the inside or skids to the outside of your curve. Since no one action must in its progress impede or conflict with another, a certain independence must prevail among the various simultaneous actions of the hands.

The chief role of the legs is to produce, maintain or increase impulsion by repetitive action of whatever form or intensity required: from taps to more or less pronounced forward shifts of the lower leg, to rapid contractions of the calf muscles; the use of the spur ranging from a mere prick to a veritable "attack." The essential is to render the horse light to the leg, to imbue it from the very first with an unquestioning respect for that particular aid: by clear actions varying in strength in accordance with the horse's nature *and while the hands yield!* Little by little you should obtain quite as much free forward movement with lighter leg action; if not, resort immediately to stronger action, then return to the gentler form, so alternating until you get what you expect. Eventually you will obtain equal impulsion by lighter action. Be sparing, however, with the use of your legs lest the horse grow numb to their constant touch. Strongly or lightly, they must speak clearly while, in the early stages, the hands must "throw open the gate" to leave no room for doubt in the young horse's mind.

The action of the single leg can produce three clearly distinct effects, depending on place and form. It can drive the haunches in the direction opposite the side of its action, can create impulsion or produce a given bend.

Slightly retracted and acting backward, the single leg (the other remaining passive and the hands refraining from opposing resistance) causes the horse to shift its haunches to the opposite side while increasing speed. The lateral shift of the croup will be relatively minor, unless on the contrary the hands oppose or slow the forward movement, significantly accentuating this shift.

Acting at the girth by light taps or forward pulsations, the single leg increases impulsion without changing the direction of the haunches.

Acting at its normal place and by a continuous perpendicular pressure, the single leg prompts a bend whose degree, while always minimal, is contingent on the horse's level of training.

The body weight can be called an aid chiefly because, properly used or unused, it will keep from disturbing the horse: for the rider must accompany his mount, neither follow nor precede the motion; that is, neither lag behind nor forge ahead. The oft repeated comparison of riding and dancing is very much to the point. A couple of ballroom dancers should convey the impression of being moved simultaneously by an outer force, while in reality only one of them takes all initiatives. By balance, relaxation and lightness the other accompanies these initiatives harmoniously, neither anticipating nor "hanging on."

Lateral work, such as the half-pass, is where the body is the most useful. As the rider leans on the stirrup on the side of the movement, this light pressure brings about a slight shift of the seat which lets him accompany the movement. But such minimal weight shifts must not entail any perceptible change of position.

The Coordination of the Aids

is the proper combination, whether simultaneous or in very close sequence, of several aids in order to obtain a given movement. If mutually helpful by the way in which they are acting, yielding and resisting, they effectively reinforce each other. In the midst of such simultaneity it is admittedly difficult to check the correctness of each individual one. Baucher remarked that all too often their coincidence causes "one of them to be blamed for another's sins," and this was indeed the rationale behind his constantly misunderstood formula "hand without legs, legs without hand," which allows us to verify the quality of each of our aids while allowing the horse to obey but to a single one at a time. Our work thereby becomes more precise, the horse progresses by simple and clear means, and in their eventual coordination the aids will remain as clear in combination as they had been separately.

V.
THE GRAMMAR OF RIDING: BALANCE

Before we continue on our way, let me express my awareness that whoever ventures to set down an actual training progression will almost surely disappoint most of those who seek advice from the printed page. The ones disdain "the grammar" of riding as being too "elementary," the others shy away from it as being too "intellectual;" both will say that no one need waste good reading time on explanations of such well-known terms as balance, or engagement, let alone impulsion. The latter will instead demand a recipe for a surefire departure at the canter, the former will clamor for a pirouette without a hitch.

Yet there are no "recipes" for horse and rider as there may be for the cook and her stew, or even for the chef and his soufflé. Yet, feel and flair, that certain extra *je ne sais quoi*, also makes the difference between the cook and the chef. While without those gifts art of any sort is unthinkable, it is, all will agree, just as unthinkable without a solid awareness of the grammar underlying the style; from prose to poetry, be it in literature, *haute cuisine* or *haute école*. Where organic matter is involved, this grammar encompasses its properties and reactions to which culinary technique must respond or fail; and this field of knowledge represents the hidden factor which makes the difference between the average and the excellent.

But unlike the honest cook, we are not dealing with an egg and a wooden spoon; not even with a single body like the ballet master whose students, nonetheless, are made to practice their grammar for years on end without arousing their or anyone's amazement, let alone impatience.

With this in mind, let us pause to discuss the nature and effects of perhaps the foremost ingredient entering into all movements of the horse, the more critically the higher you go: **Balance.** A clear understanding of it will preserve your green horse, and guarantee its genuine progress as well as your own by helping you to cope with the increasing problems inherent in advanced equitation.

I think that you will be interested in a little-known, yet quite conclusive experiment relating to weight distribution as carried out in the nineteenth century by no less a man than François Baucher.

He and a General Morris, a specialist in equine science, were curious to see just exactly how much influence head and neck action exerted on a horse's four legs, most specifically the fore and hind bipeds. They went to the Paris customs office which possessed twin scales of recent invention used, it must be assumed, for weighing cattle. They had brought along a mare which they placed with her forelegs on the center of one, her hindlegs on the center of the other. Both scales being equal in size and on exactly the same level, the two surfaces acted not unlike the plates of an ordinary scale.

The mare, somewhat heavy in head and neck but otherwise normally constituted, remained saddled and bridled. Completely immobile, her head held in a for her normal (rather low than high) position, she showed the following results on the scales:

Forehand	Quarters	Total Weight	Surplus on Forehand
210 kg	174 kg	384 kg	36 kg

♦

The weight fluctuated by 3 to 5 kg between forehand and quarters because of the visceral movements occasioned by the mere act of breathing!

When, head lowered to the point where her nose remained at chest level, the mare was once more immobile, 8 kg went from quarters to forehand.

Forehand	Quarters	Total Weight	Surplus on Forehand
218 kg	166 kg	384 kg	52 kg

♦

Head raised to where the nose reached withers level, 10 kg passed from the motionless mare's forehand to her quarters.

Forehand	Quarters	Total Weight	Surplus on Forehand
200 kg	184 kg	384 kg	16 kg

♦

When her head was returned to its normal position and drawn by the snaffle bit backward toward the neck and slightly upward, 8 kg passed to the quarters.

Forehand	Quarters	Total Weight	Surplus on Forehand
202 kg	182 kg	384 kg	20 kg

◆

"These results," the general tells us, "prove that the higher the head is carried, either by nature or by hand action, the more evenly its weight and that of the neck is distributed over the legs, provided this position is not obtained by force."

When Baucher mounted the mare which was once more placed in the initial attitude, the scales showed the following results:

Forehand	Quarters	Total Weight	Surplus on Forehand
251 kg	197 kg	448 kg	54 kg

◆

"In an academic position, " quoth the general, "the rider's 64 kg weight thus rested by 41 kg on the forehand, by 23 kg on the quarters."

When Baucher leaned back, 10 more kg went to the quarters, and when he drew back the mare's head after his own method, another 8 kg (i.e., a total of 18 kg) flowed backward, as follows:

Forehand	Quarters	Total Weight	Surplus on Forehand
233 kg	215 kg	448 kg	18 kg

◆

When he supported himself exclusively on his stirrups, the forehand found itself weighed down by an additional 12 kg.

With some minor and foreseeable differences due to conformation, the same experiment with a rather misshapen grey led to a similar result.

The same Baucher's tenet that "balance must be obtained without interference with movement while, on the other hand, movement in the act of being produced must not interfere with balance" appears to be at first sight, if not a truism, the clear statement of a logical imperative. On closer examination, however, there arises the basic problem that the overall attitude of, say, a horse at a full gallop is quite different from that of a horse in *haute école*. One need not be a horseman to realize that a horse must be in perfect balance in order to clear a mighty steeplechase fence but that this balance is totally different from the no less perfect one of the horse in the dressage ring.

In movement (the only point of constant interest to us, since equitation is by definition movement!), balance is contingent on far more than the elevation of the neck and the *ramener*,* because "balance in movement is the relation between alternate losses of and returns to balance in the course of locomotion. When the losses predominate in this sequence, the horse is on the forehand, in the opposite case he is on the haunches." (Maj. Licart)

What means of intervention does the rider have in this matter? Depending on his purpose and the sort of equitation practiced, he may act on both ends of the horse (head, neck and haunches), or practically on the haunches alone. Whatever he does, participation of the haunches is of the essence.

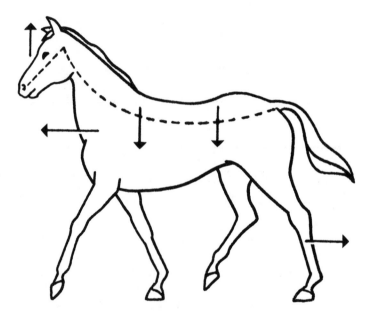

Fig. 5. The neck is raised, the back is hollow, the hindlegs do not engage, the horse is cock-throated and on the forehand (see page 27).

---

*The *ramener* is a near-vertical head position assumed through the flexion of the first two cervical vertebrae. It is said to be complete when the head is held strictly vertical, but it must not ever go behind this line; if it does, the horse is overbent, a grievous fault.

While the scales have proved the influence of head and neck position on the horse's balance at the halt, once he is in motion weight distribution ceases to be constant, not only because of the alternation of loss and regaining of balance, but because of the engagement factor. The farther the hindlegs engage under the mass, the more of its weight do they assume, lightening the forehand to the same extent.

Extreme elevation of the neck—head at the horizontal and without previous suppling to allow the joints of the quarters to flex—will force the horse to hollow his back, causing the withers to collapse and the hindlegs to spraddle, thus virtually paralyzing the paces. For is it not a well-known fact that the rider's best defense against a bucking horse is to raise his neck to the utmost?!

The forehand can be lightened only by associating the work on the quarters with the *combined* elevation of the neck and *ramener*, albeit in proportions corresponding to the horse's conformation, notably to the set-on of his neck at shoulder level.

The engagement of the hindlegs of a horse in racing is far more pronounced than that of the dressage horse at the piaffe, but the *haute école* horse's forehand is lightened through the reflux of weight onto the quarters caused by the elevation of the neck in combination with the *ramener*, the flexibility of the hindquarter joints allowing that part to accept the surplus. Also, the slower movements of a dressage horse require a far lesser play of his neck, particularly at the trot, than is the case for the racehorse straining to the limit of his capacities, and you can clearly observe the jockeys' technique in encouraging the horses' use of their necks.

Between these two extremes we have the show jumper who, mentally and physically prepared to respond willingly and easily to his rider's demands, must be able to make fast and frequent changes of speed, direction and balance. In show jumping balance is vital, speed essential. In dressage speed varies with the length of stride, but the rhythm within one and the same pace must remain the same. In show jumping, on the contrary, when obliged to reduce length of stride, one chooses at times to accelerate the rhythm to prevent loss of speed.

The jumper rebalances himself principally through increased engagement, with or without raising his neck. Under proper impulsion and speed, combined hand and leg action will bring about a change of rhythm without affecting the speed. With the dressage horse the problem is rather reversed. At the extended trot he overtracks, the neck stretches, the head/neck angle opens. When passing into the collected trot he under-tracks slightly, raises his head, arches his neck, closes the head/neck angle. Since rhythm must remain the same, speed will decrease.

Just so, the closing of the hindleg joints will differ: due to the flexion of his loins the jumper's hindlegs will advance under the mass farther than those of the dressage horse whose loins flex to a far lesser degree, particularly at the trot. In any case, balance changes are fewer and smaller in dressage than in show jumping because of the obvious differences in the type and speed of the work.

Whatever influence the dressage rider can exert on his horse's balance by weight shifts of his own, the movements of his upper body must remain imperceptible to the eye, while the show jumping rider can use them to the full. You might compare the variations of equilibrium in the two disciplines to the oscillations of two different types of scale: one may weigh fractions of ounces, the other pounds, but the weight shown by each must be right.

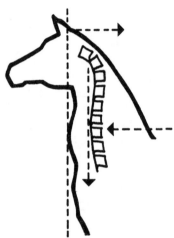

Fig. 6. The raising of the neck alone causes the first of the cervical vertebrae to retreat and to push the others downward; the horse becomes cock-throated. After a sketch from *Equitation Académique* by Gen. Decarpentry.

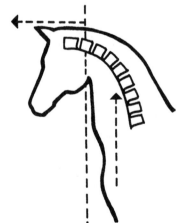

Fig. 7. The raising of the neck combined with a corresponding *ramener* draws, on the contrary, the first cervical vertebrae forward; these in turn draw the others upward. After a sketch from *Equitation Académique* by Gen. Decarpentry.

As mentioned above, the near-horizontal position of the head brought about by the sole raising of the neck will cause the poll to push the cervical vertebrae back and down, render the horse cock-throated in movement and put him on the forehand. Although during the raising, you might say, there will be a weight transfer from forehand to quarters, it is true for only the brief duration of the ongoing movement, and this at the cost of ruining the withers, the back and the paces. When, on the contrary, the neck is raised just slightly, head close to the vertical, the first cervical vertebrae are drawn forward, carrying the others upward, the upper neck muscles stretch, as, in the process, do those of the back.

That is indeed the region requiring particular attention when you buy a horse. For good balance, neck orientation must be at about 45 degrees above the horizontal, where it emerges from the shoulders. For there are deceptive necks, and they are the worst, rather high along their upper two-thirds, but low at the base, rendering it difficult, sometimes impossible, to have a horse truly framed between your reins. Look therefore principally at the base of the neck.

A horse has of course two opposite but equally effective ways of evading true *ramener*. He may go above the bit and throw back his neck, or he may overbend. In either case he denies you control over the base of his neck which is, so to speak, the foundation on which must be built all your work with respect to the neck. Its disposition largely determines the functioning of the other parts and, consequently, of the paces. Correct

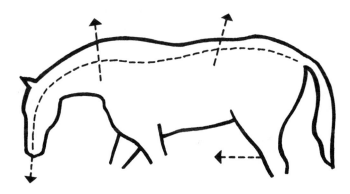

Fig. 8. As the neck is being stretched, its base rises, the topline becomes rounded, the hindlegs engage easily, and the horse is in balance.

neck and head carriage will not be achieved by legs pushing the horse onto rigid hands, but on the contrary by methodical elongation, neck stretching, lateral flexions; a left flexion bringing about an elongation on the right, assuming this to be the side to be suppled.

Once such preparatory work has been completed with the decontracting flexions at the poll, you may begin to think of *ramener* now certain to be implanted on a neck bent in the proper direction. By way of utter simplification, make this comparison: A flexible but perfectly *straight* rod, as it gives when pushed perpendicularly against a wall, may become rounded indiscriminately above or below. But if this rod is already, say, somewhat *concave* above, the push can only increase this state, and your rod must first of all be stretched, then bent slightly in the opposite direction.

The *ramener* must be in proper proportion to the neck elevation. The lower the neck carriage, the more liable you are to have an overbent horse. If, on the other hand, the neck is raised excessively, you are almost sure to end up with a star gazer. Everything therefore depends on a well-considered combination of all factors.

With the dressage horse, the *ramener* proper, easy to obtain, is rather more a consequence of an elastically held-up forehand than of the head position in itself. With the *ramener* achieved on a well-placed neck, your horse, by his willing, easy flexing at the poll, will prove to you that he is relaxed; and once this has been achieved, *and not before*, you may go on to suppling exercises which, as everyone knows, can be effectively carried out only in a state of relaxation.

We will from time to time return to such notes on "the grammar of riding," although I do not intend to get involved in pseudo-scientific speculations, including such hotly debated questions as the elusive center of gravity, which, as we just have seen, changes even on the immobile horse "because of the visceral movements occasioned by the mere act of breathing." Too much "science," while convincing on paper, fails on the back of a horse.

VI.
FLEXIONS

The system of flexions is the only surefire one not only to supple but relax a horse; only in that state can he move in perfect balance, so to become a truly good ride. It also allows for more effective utilization of animals of poor or mediocre conformation.

Before such work can start, however, you must accustom your horse to contact with the whip by sliding it along his neck, caressingly along his back, speaking to him in a gentle tone of voice. This done, he will remain calm and trusting when lightly tapped on the breast, as shall happen in your initial exercises on foot.

A horse will obviously relax more readily at slow paces, and what could be "slower" than the halt? The only risk you might incur is seeing him evade your demand by backing up. You cannot counteract this risk on foot, but you can prevent it by previous teaching. Here is how:

Place your horse alongside a wall, stand on his left, next to his head, facing his quarters, your left hand grasping both snaffle reins behind his mouth, the right holding the whip. Now tap him lightly on the breast, along with a slight forward traction by the reins and a click of the tongue. Although in a first reflex he will step back, tact and patience will soon teach him to move forward. Should you encounter inordinate difficulty with free forward movement, get an aide with a lunging whip to stand sideways and in back, where the horse can see both him and the movements of the whip which however should never touch him. Thus even on foot can you prompt and control the forward movement and at that point only may you begin work on flexions.

One too often uses the words "stiff" and "tense" as though interchangeable, while the first denotes a physical, the second, a mental state. Suppleness in a horse does not exclude contraction at neck and mouth. Simple gymnastic movements can remedy this state, *if performed under relaxed conditions.* This much for the *mental* aspect. *Physically,* a horse's conformation is often far from ideal, particularly as regards neck and set-on of the head. To an extent such defects can be remedied by flexions stretching the various neck muscles, all practiced in the early stages, though certain ones are soon discontinued, others emphasized. If your horse rather tends to overbend, beware of accentuating this tendency by insisting on the flexion of the *ramener* which would only aggravate it. If he tends rather to go above the bit, avoid upward flexions. This is to say, whatever you are about to do at any time, keep your horse's conformation in mind, do not overstep his natural capabilities. And in this particular case, do not forget that since he has two ends, **flexions at the forehand must be accompanied by flexions at the quarters.**

A horse may thwart his rider's intent by means of either neck or quarters. The neck, in particular, plays a determining part: a prone horse cannot rise while his head is kept pressed to the ground. The logical inference is that, with loss of the use of his neck, he loses the ability to resist and that, therefore, domination of the neck is vital for control. Since, notwithstanding, he can stiffen his jaw to neutralize the effect of your hand on his neck, it is with his jaw that your work must begin.

The flexions of the neck, raising or stretching it forward and downward, are preceded by flexions at the jaw and followed by lateral and direct flexions. Lateral flexions are for the front of the horse what the half-turns on the forehand are for the back; direct flexions correspond to the rein back which has a suppling effect on back and loins.

Since, aside from their suppling action, these exercises are powerful means of domination, they also are rather dangerous and their practice requires great discernment. The trainer must be experienced enough to know which should be emphasized, which should be played down and which should not be employed. He must, moreover, be possessed of both innate and acquired equestrian tact, a somewhat rare commodity. Nothing is, we know, as dangerous as a little learning, but even an experienced trainer might fall into the trap of blithely and fragmentarily applying what may have been but a casual discovery on his part.

Flexions are useful in training for all equestrian disciplines because, on the flat as well as over fences, a relaxed horse performs incomparably better than one that is tense. Yielding laterally, he will save his energies for what he is about rather than waste them in fighting his rider.

On Foot

Without the encumbrance of your weight, your horse will understand and respond to your demands better and more quickly; you yourself will benefit from your ability to see him; and your hand, closer to his mouth, will act more clearly and effectively. So begin your work on foot.

Flexions at the Jaw

Stand left of your horse's neck, facing front, the left snaffle rein in your right hand, your left hand bringing over the right rein, below his neck, at four to five inches from his mouth. Now gently draw your wrists in opposite directions, thus compressing the lower jaw as with a slipknot. Do not exert force. If obedience is not immediately forthcoming, wait without increasing or decreasing this action, for the horse to open his mouth. At this signal of his yielding, you too must immediately yield. Pat him to convey that this is exactly what you had expected and keep in mind that such recognition must be forthcoming throughout, and in all exercises.

Should your horse fail to react to several such attempts, you may try a rather more powerful means to assure the opening of the mouth, provided you subsequently return to the classical method! Stand facing him, left rein in your right hand, right rein in the left, at about four inches from his mouth. Your hands will exert rein tension in opposite directions: right rein backward, left rein forward, yielding as soon as the mouth has opened. Pat your horse, then start over; now left rein backward, right one forward. Whether things come easily or not, frequent lessons are preferable to long ones; whatever the work, demand little at a time but demand often.

Lateral Flexions of the Neck

Once your horse yields easily in his mouth, you may go on to laterally flexing his neck. Stand by his left point of the shoulder; acting in the direction of his mouth, your right hand passes the right rein across the base of his neck, your left hand grasps the left rein about four inches from his mouth; then you exert a light and even pressure on both sides. As soon as the horse yields, you raise your left hand, place the left rein in a vertical position, touching his cheek, while your right hand increases its action, drawing his head to the right. No sooner have you obtained the slightest bend of the neck to the right than you must yield and reward. Start over, reversing your aids, from the left side, to obtain a flexion to the left.

It is vitally important for the horse to yield in his mouth before the flexion and to keep it relaxed throughout. The poll must remain the supreme

Fig. 9. The crossed snaffle reins are held at 4 inches from the horse's mouth. Neither increasing nor decreasing their tension, the trainer is waiting for the horse to yield, as witnessed by the half-opening of his mouth. Rein tension must be moderate and, above all, constant, and hand action must cease as soon as the horse yields.

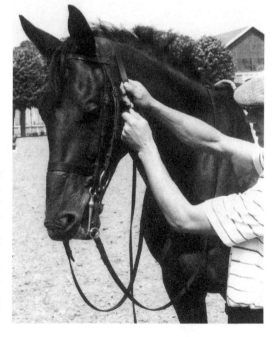

Fig. 10. A second method: the right snaffle rein is placed across the poll and the right hand acts downward toward the mouth while the left, holding the left rein, is acting upward toward the right hand. Both actions must be equal in intensity and, as in the previous exercise, must maintain an even tension until the horse mobilizes his jaw.

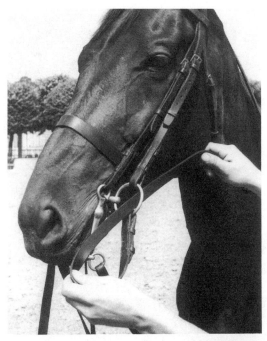

Figs. 11 & 12. By a third method, one places the center of the snaffle rein on top of the poll, slips one rein into each snaffle ring, letting the rein attachments pivot around the rings. As the trainer's hand is acting toward the horse's ears, the snaffle bit acts vertically on the corners of the mouth which thereupon slightly opens.

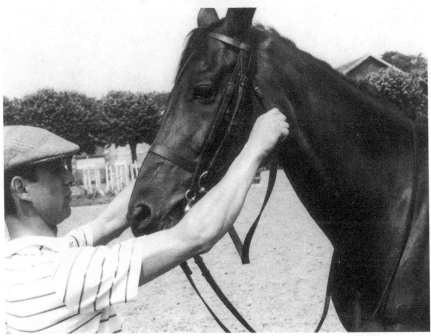

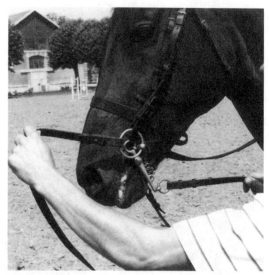

Figs. 13 & 14. By a fourth method, the horse is made to yield on one side (on the left in the photo), then on the other, and eventually by the use of both curb reins. The snaffle rein will keep the head in place; the curb rein will prompt the slight opening of the mouth. All of these exercises are performed in the pursuit of this movement as slight as that produced in the act of swallowing.

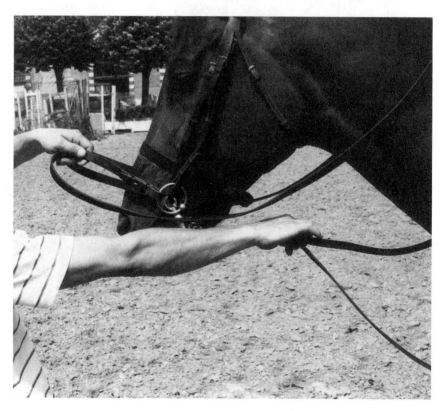

point of the neck. Since the area to be suppled is close to the head, beware of overflexing the neck, provoking a break at about mid-neck, a state more disastrous even than having an exceedingly rigid neck. Head position must remain vertical during the flexion, so make certain when flexing laterally to the right that its lower part is not drawn to that side, the upper part thus leaning to the left. This would let the horse evade the suppling effect, and it is your left hand which, aside from regulating the action of the right, must keep his head at the vertical. From its somewhat rigid base, the well-prepared neck should show increasing suppleness as it rises to meet the head.

Fig. 15. Lateral Flexion at the Neck. The right snaffle rein is placed across the neck near the withers. Following a direct flexion, right rein action draws the head to the right, while the left hand acts in the direction of the ears, thus maintaining the head in a vertical position at the proper height. Reverse aids prompt a flexion to the left.

Direct Flexions

The purpose here is to place the horse's head in a nearly vertical position where the bit will act most effectively. Moreover, a direct flexion at the poll combined with a relaxed jaw is material proof of a general state of relaxation rendering your horse submissive and ready to perform at your command.

Facing him, grasp the separated reins close to the bit. By raising them, you raise his head, careful not to let him back up. If he does, stop the flexion, make him step forward and start over. The elevation must be obtained with due regard for his conformation and, as in whatever you do, without undue initial demands. His head at the proper height, you work your reins horizontally, keeping contact with the mouth and, if necessary, mobilizing your fingers to effect some vibrations. He will begin by relaxing at the jaw, then flex at the poll. Do not, in response to an initial attempt or two, expect a complete flexion bringing the head to the vertical, which only comes with repetition. Above all, remember that flexions in general, and this one in particular, are the result of relaxation, never of forceful action.

Fig. 16. Direct Flexion at the Poll. The right snaffle rein passing across the neck near the withers, the left hand acts more or less in the direction of the right, controlling the height of the head, raising it by moving upward, lowering it by moving downward. Following relaxation at the jaw, mere finger pressure on the reins will produce a yielding at the poll.

Provided the direct flexion is preceded by a proper elevation of the head, there is no risk of overbending or of yielding at nearly mid-neck. To understand the extent of damage caused by overbending, think of a horse's "broken" neck as of a garden hose slashed between faucet and nozzle. Like the stream of water, the impulsion can no longer reach your hand in full. Proper head position is determined by its elevation and the direct flexion at the poll which must remain the highest point of the neck. This elevation must be such that the bars, which are subjected to the action of the bit, are situated at a horizontal passing at about the upper third of the chest. By such a head carriage, the horse's mass in its entirety is affected by the rider's hand, however light its action, and the hand in turn receives the slightest forward shift of the horse's weight.

Neck-stretching Flexions

Stretching here causes the crest muscles to yield. Stand by the horse's neck, facing forward, take the right rein in your left hand, the left in your right, crossed behind the horse's chin and four inches away from the mouth. Moving your hands apart, exert downward pressure. After a moment, he will lower his head as he relaxes at the jaw. At the early state, be content with little, but eventually you must bring his head down very low. Do not forget to reward the slightest manifestation of obedience as though it were total submission, for these vague hints point straight to your goal.

Fig. 17. Downward Flexion. The snaffle reins are crossed behind the mouth and the horse is made to relax his jaw. This obtained, the hands act downward.

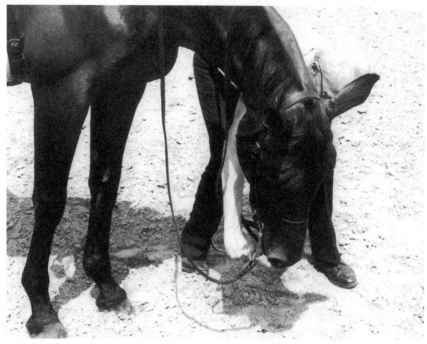

Fig. 18. Downward Flexion. While even tentative obedience should initially be rewarded, by and by the point must be reached where the horse's mouth closely approaches the ground. The trainer's hands must feel the relaxation of the neck muscles as well as obtain a mollification of the jaws. For this suppling exercise to be complete, the horse should be walked without raising his mouth from the ground.

Figs. 19 & 20. Upward Flexion. The hands are acting on the snaffle rein alternately in the direction of the ears in order to raise the head, with due regard for the horse's conformation and most particularly for the orientation of his neck from its set-on. Having obtained this slight elevation, the trainer prompts a direct flexion at the poll. Results will be achieved by frequent repetition rather than by any strong demand. While both positions shown here will be effective, the one shown in figure 19 is safest for the trainer. ▶

19

20

Half-Pirouette in Reverse (half-turn on the forehand)

Rotation of the quarters around the forehand—first on foot, then under saddle—leads to control over the haunches and therewith over the engagement of the hindlegs. It also makes for superior impulsion and a stricter and more efficient control of direction.

Face the croup, take both reins in your left hand, four inches from the horse's mouth, your right hand holding a long but not overly flexible dressage whip. As this comes in contact with the horse's left flank, reinforced if necessary by a few clicks of the tongue, he will advance. Apply this touch just as the left hind rises, your left hand prompting a slowdown *without interruption of the walk.* He will respond to this combined action by taking a step aside to the right, the left hind advancing *across* the right. A few more such steps are repeated on the other side, working more intensively on the stiffer one.

Figs. 21 & 22. The Half-Turn on the Forehand. The use of the whip on the horse's legs is teaching him to shift his haunches. Initially, as here, the trainer is making use of the rein on the side of the whip action.

21

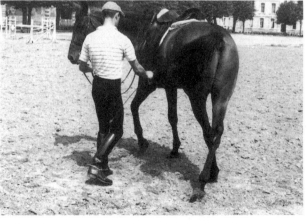

22

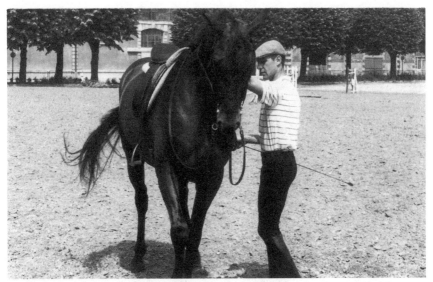

Fig. 23. Later, as shown here, the horse's head is turned rather in the opposite direction.

Rein Back

Facing the horse, grasp the right rein with your left hand, the left one with your right. Raise the head and prompt a direct flexion. Head placed relatively high, alternate hand action will obtain one or two backward steps. Be careful to keep the horse straight and, by a click of the tongue, to follow this up with an immediate forward step.

Once your horse has been confirmed in this work in hand, the same will be done under saddle.

Under Saddle

Direct Flexions and Relaxing at the Jaw

Your hands assure their perfect steadiness by resting, on quite short reins, rather low alongside the neck, their exact height obviously depending on the nature of your horse. Finger mobility alone, without hand intervention, should prompt the flexion because, accustomed to this exercise in hand, the horse should respond easily. As soon as he flexes, yield, but keep prolonging the time of flexion, first for a few seconds at the walk, by and by longer, eventually at the trot and canter. In every instance, confirm him at one pace before proceeding to the faster one.

Fig. 24. Direct Flexion. Simple finger pressure on the reins, without advance or retraction of the hands, will cause the horse to yield at the poll. At an early stage the hands should be placed as low as may be necessary for the horse's clearest understanding.

Lateral Flexions

Example, flexing to the right: feel out your horse's mouth on both reins, then draw his head to the right while your left hand regulates the movement and applies the left rein vertically against his cheek to avoid a tilt of his head, which must remain at the vertical rather than nose pointing right, ears to the left. Work, as always, on both sides and more intensively on the difficult one. For a slight flexion, do the same at the walk; for a more pronounced one, shift both hands to the left, keeping contact with both reins. Neck bent to the right, the horse will nonetheless continue to travel straight. Proceed likewise at the trot.

Again remember that, since the poll must be the upmost point of the neck, the head must previously be raised satisfactorily.

Fig. 25. Lateral Flexion. Following a direct flexion accompanied by a yielding at the jaw, a slow traction on the right rein draws the head to the right, while the left hand is raised to maintain the head vertically at the proper height. Reverse aids obtain a flexion to the left.

Flexions by Descent of the Neck

Hold both hands above the horse's ears, exerting upward tension on both reins. Trying to escape the discomfort, the horse will presently lower his neck and your fingers must yield, but not lose contact. Repeat this exercise at the trot.

Fig. 26. Neck Stretching. At the beginning of the stretch.

Fig. 27. Neck Stretching. At the end of the stretch.

Fig. 28. Neck Stretching. The position of the hand determines the direction: downward and forward, as shown on figures 26 and 27, or downward only as shown here. In all cases, the fingers must yield without losing contact.

Fig. 29. Downward Flexion. The reins are held, quite long, in the left hand close to the trainer's chest while the outer edge of his right hand, posed on the reins, weighs down on them. The horse flexes.

Fig. 30. Upward Flexion. Alternately and as far to the fore as possible, the hands are acting upward on the reins and, once the head has been somewhat raised, descend to prompt a direct flexion without, however, causing a consequent descent of the horse's poll.

Rein back

Once the neck has been properly raised, rein backs prompted by finger pressure on the reins alone will contribute to flexing the quarter joints and thereby improving the balance.

Never employ force or constraint in this work which should rely exclusively on the mobility of your fingers. In no other way will you get your horse to relax, and only a relaxed horse can be effectively suppled.

VII.
First Work Under Saddle

The Mounting Lesson

Having achieved what we expected from lunging work, we now acquaint the horse with the feel of saddle and bit, beginning with just a roller on his back to be tightened only in the course of the lesson once he has ceased to be tense.

Two or three days later we put on the saddle, without stirrups to avoid the small noise these would make beating against the flaps which, for similar reasons, are held down by a surcingle. We girth just enough to keep the saddle from shifting, a bit later to check whether a little more is required. Usually the horse bucks or lashes out a bit at first; if you drive him forward at the trot such capers will come to an end.

The following day it will be time for the bit. As discussed earlier, I definitely prefer the Baucher snaffle. Entwine the reins so they will exert a little tension on the snaffle, secure them by slipping the throatlatch through them, and place the cavesson over the bridle. Lunge him this way for a few days; individual horses can be more or less difficult. The idea is, at any stage of training, not ever to surprise a horse: always to require a single new thing at a time and never to take a step ahead before the preceding one has been assimilated.

The mounting lesson may take either of two forms, both sharing one imperative: they must be imparted at the end of a lunging session. They also share one purpose: to impress on the horse from the very start that he must not move during mounting. I will describe in some detail the procedure where the trainer works without assistance, the way I personally prefer.

Give the stirrup leather a few tugs, then let it lightly hit the saddle. Take the reins, the right a bit shorter than the left, and mount in the normal fashion, grasping the saddle not by the cantle but just behind the right flap. Though many think, wrongly, that one should rise by the right hand's pull toward the body, this pull should come from the left hand grasping mane; the right, quite to the contrary, must push down vertically to keep the saddle from turning. And beware of touching the horse with the left toe as you swing your right leg over!

While going through these motions, continue to speak to your horse. Should he move, put him back, to stand straight, in exactly the original spot, and start over from scratch; we do not want to take him by surprise. We return him, never brusquely but stubbornly, to the very same place in order to make him understand that moving is forbidden. Mounting and dismounting should indeed be effected on the center line, impressing upon the horse that this is the place where immobility is imperative.

You will of course sit down as lightly as you can and the twist given the right stirrup leather before mounting lets your right foot find the iron even before you begin to ease yourself down. Once in the saddle, both feet in the stirrups, reins adjusted, request by a click of the tongue the forward movement *straight ahead.*

Be content with two to four minutes at the walk before returning to the center line; a halt at the voice, dismount and return him to the stables. This most important lesson must be given with patience and firmness, with as many repetitions as necessary, insisting on absolute immobility at mounting and dismounting. No matter how smoothly this first lesson may be going, do not ask for more than those few minutes at the walk.

Besides the usual lunging, this will be your only work for the next few days: improving each day the results of the preceding one, only gradually lengthening the time spent at the walk. Remember to reward and stop in good time lest your horse react as any human would if asked ever to give a little more than he has just willingly given.

On the other hand, never be satisfied with a mere "just about;" the mounting lesson in fact is hard to give, but it can be done. You must realize that it is designed to obtain *the very first act of submission* on the part of the *mounted* horse, so that we must return to it each and any time submissiveness appears to falter. If you allow him to move ever so slightly —be it from fear or surprise rather than ill will, a distinction not always easily made—his fine memory will register the fact; he will conclude that, immobility being after all only relative, the rider will be quite happy with just relative obedience.

He has already learned about immobility for three, four or five seconds on the lungeline, and immobility, though in a different framework, is now demanded. If, incidentally, you suspect that your own awkwardness sometimes causes him to fidget, use a trained horse to improve your technique. If still unsure, you might prefer the second fashion earlier alluded to which differs from the above only by the use of cavesson and lungeline. A difficult or impatient horse will be called back to order by a few shakes of the line. Both ways have their adepts and their pros and cons. To my mind, if the lunging lessons have been well done, if the horse has been granted time to get used to the girth, then to the saddle and finally to the bridle, if one has known how to gain his trust and gives this mounting lesson to a relaxed horse at the end of a lunging session, the first of the two procedures is best. In any event, after two or three lessons of the second type you must progress to the first.

Aside from continued work on the lungeline, though shorter by half, you will now ride on the track both at the walk and the rising trot. The main purpose of the trot in these early lessons under saddle is to relax the horse as well as to add some variety to the work at the walk.

In Quest of Free Forward Movement

During the first year of training it is preferable for both horse and rider—and easier for the latter—to do without spurs. For the horse the whiplash is a mightier driving agent than the prick of the spur; for the rider there is safety in the improbability of using the whip inadvertently, which well may happen with the spur.

Making the horse go forward may indeed be the first problem one needs to overcome, which can be done in various ways. If clicks of the tongue do not suffice, add leg action as earlier explained. If that won't do, add the whip, applied as close as possible behind your leg. This failing, or if the horse lashes out behind, have someone with a lunging whip stand behind and visible to him on the inner track; only of course to encourage him by its sight. As a last resource return to lunging lessons, although now rider up, using the opening rein with caution to avoid backward traction in changes of direction. Since you want the rein tension to be produced as laterally as possible in the desired direction, exaggerate the hand and arm gesture while your legs and the clicks of your tongue are prompting a speedup.

For halts, effected on the track, make your weight come to bear on the ends of the reins, which means keeping your elbows close to the body, closing your fingers, straightening up and blocking your shoulders, your voice joining in the demands of your hand. As soon as the halt has materialized you must yield by diminishing rein tension and, furthermore, not ask for more than two or three seconds of immobility. If the horse moves, the hands act as though requesting another halt, then yield. To be effective, this yielding must occur at the very instant of the halt and during which you yourself must remain immobile. One often moves without realizing it. Also, prepare your horse for the halt by ceasing all impulsive aids in the first place, then progressively slowing down by alternately closing the fingers of right and left hand. If none of this will prompt a halt, use a calm but forthright opening rein by the outside hand which will put him nose to the wall: anything rather than backward traction.

Since at the outset the meaning of leg action as a producer of forward movement is unfamiliar to the horse, it must be explained to him by association with already familiar agents: the riding or lunging whip. This "lesson of the legs" must be given calmly but clearly, the force of the whiplash commensurate with the sensitivity of the horse, yet strong enough to make him understand that you are determined to get what you are looking for.

So place both reins in one hand and the whip, pointing upward, in the other. Use both legs and *immediately* apply the whip just behind your leg, remembering to advance the bridle hand so the horse won't run up against it. Let him canter on for about 100 feet, pat him, then gradually slow him down to a walk. Take two or three turns around the school on a loose rein before starting over and do not forget the patting. Surely, when on the next occasion the legs will act alone, the horse will move forward freely. This lesson must be repeated whenever you feel him growing sluggish.

Remember, however, that the early difficulties in making the horse advance under saddle are natural ones, mounted work making unwonted demands upon his back, his mouth and thereby on his neck. For two reasons our weight deprives him of his former ease in using his back for locomotion: his back muscles are still weak and our weight changes his balance because, in a normal position, two thirds of our body weighs on the forehand, one third only on the quarters. The horse's natural reflex is therefore to retain his impulsive forces.

As concerns the neck, which he uses almost constantly when at liberty, most particularly in changing his balance, the presence of the bridle considerably limits both the frequency and the extent of such movements. At best (that is, under a light hand), then, he will be somewhat suspicious of the bit, the more so if driven onto it before he has acquired a minimum of trust in your hand. From fear of getting hurt, he will limit as much as possible those neck movements which he actually needs in order to find the new balance required by the addition of your weight. Therefore give maximum freedom to the neck, yet without losing contact with the mouth, if only minimal, until the horse has learned to trust your hand.

In Quest of Contact

The matter of contact greatly affects not only the mouth, the neck and the back, but the functioning of the hindlegs. The extent of a horse's neck movements, varying in accordance with the pace, are least ample at the trot. For permanent contact with the mouth without interference with the neck, your hand, and in the early stages your arms, must accompany its movements smoothly, effecting slowdowns and halts only progressively by limiting the motion gradually. Hand opposition is beneficial only after the muscles have been shaped and the joints suppled. Premature attempts to collect an insufficiently suppled or relaxed horse are self-defeating. Such hand opposition impedes the play of the back and quarters. In the early stages, it is all important to permit the neck to move to the greatest possible extent if one wishes to extend the stride to the utmost and to encourage the horse to reach for the bit.

Neck Stretching

Many things are achieved by this single exercise, because it works the muscles of the topline and therewith strengthens both the back and the neck, the latter notably at its base. It also serves the mobility and engagement of the hindlegs, and teaches the horse (not the least of its advantages!) to trust our hand and therefore to reach for the bit, all of which is instrumental for free forward movement. Although not an absolute must, neck stretching spares most riders certain early difficulties with which they may not be able to cope without spoiling their horses' paces in the process.

The final aim is not, of course, to have the horse go sniffing the sawdust, but rather to raise his neck. Yet this goal will subsequently be reached with far less risk if the neck has previously been muscled at its base. In building a house, does one not work downward to dig the foundations before erecting the walls thereon?

If you have ever trotted a young horse on a normally adjusted rein while driving him onto the bit and then done likewise and without a change in your leg action under the effect of neck stretching, you must have felt the back move far more distinctly, because more amply, under your seat. With the consequent help of the back during this exercise, the play of the hindlegs will be improved and rendered better able to drive the forehand. Free and indeed encouraged to use his neck, the horse moves forward more freely, without the rider losing contact with the mouth. (See Figures 26-28.)

Holding your hands high, practically above the horse's ears, you maintain continuous rein tension until, after a moment, he will try to escape the discomfort by stretching and lowering head and neck. Some horses yield more readily at the halt, others at the walk. What is important is to yield at the horse's first incipient gesture, rather than expect him to move as distinctly and completely as would one trained to this exercise, and to yield during the stretch without losing contact with the mouth.

Once this works well, the same is obtained by "combing (or 'stroking') the reins;" that is, by sliding one hand backward on the reins, the other taking over as the first reaches the end of its run. Be sure to use plain reins, none else will do. Take both, separated by your index finger near the neck; for example, in the right hand which you slide backward, rein tension determined by the degree to which your fingers close. As this hand reaches mid-course, get ready to have the other follow, and so forth. The proper height for your hands and the tension to be exerted are yours to find by trial and error. Some horses require very light, others rather strong tension. By no means be content with a stretch now and then; it must come to be produced at every first demand. All this is just preparatory for the real work, done at the rising trot, on straight lines, circles or elements thereof, subsequently over poles on the ground, eventually over cavaletti.

This "natural" neck stretching is in many ways preferable to such mechanical means as the chambon which, though it yields automatically when the horse does, cannot encourage contact with the bit. Many a horse actually avoids such contact in order to escape the corrective action which the gear is designed to effect. He trots head down, neck stretched, unable to change position, while on your hand he stretches, then returns to the normal head and neck carriage until you demand another stretch. For what is of interest above all else is the *repetition*, not the position but the *movement*.

Two objections are sometimes voiced:

1. That this exercise teaches the horse to pull the reins from the rider's hands; true only if the trainer fails to make it clear to him that combing the reins means "stretch!" while holding them separated means "neck and head at their normal place." If any initiative taken by the horse is in all instances sternly opposed, he will be quick to understand the difference.

2. That it puts the horse on the forehand. First of all, not really that much because, though at the halt only the head and neck position have any bearing on weight distribution, in movement this ceases to hold true. Here the engagement is an important factor which virtually counterbalances the rest.

At this early stage the free development of the paces is in fact paramount because it is the prime element in helping the horse to find and improve his balance under the rider.

VIII.
The Neck Rein:
When and How

Before you continue your progression, remember this: you do not expect a child to act like an adult; you do not teach him mathematics before he can count. And yet one tends to act this way in training a horse. One also expects him to have too long an attention span. After five or six minutes of work he needs a brief respite during which nothing is demanded. Horses, like people, do well only what they enjoy. If leaving his box means, rather than a series of unpleasant demands, physical exercise without undue fatigue and a reward for every show of good will, the same type of work done gaily rather than tediously will produce superior results. However, your horse must also be made to feel, from the start, that his well-being is contingent on his attentive obedience. Failing this, do ask yourself whether your demand was not beyond his understanding or physical ability. If not, keep repeating it, patiently, until you get what you want. The occasional tidbit in the course of a lesson seems to have gone out of fashion, which is a great pity; for it is far more clever to have the horse associate sweets with his lessons than with the stables: rest needs no sweetener.

The basic rules above are invariable, but horses' characters are not. Timid ones need their rider's help in acquiring self-confidence. Those of a playful nature require a certain firmness to temper their spirit of independence. Some tend to be sad or nervous. Are they eating properly? What can be the matter with them? Remember that young horses are more impressionable than those who have already seen a thing or two. Everything, absolutely everything, enters into the picture if one does not want to see a horse, to quote Monsieur de Pluvinel, *"perdre sa fleur et sa gentillesse"* (shed its kindness and its bloom).

School horses work far too much; the privately owned leave their stalls for just an hour or two per day and maybe only once a week for a hack. Having mostly four walls for one's horizon is not the best way to encourage *joie de vivre*, let alone impulsion. One cannot dwell too much on the necessity to ride out as often as possible, in fact every and any time weather allows. Our main purpose here is indeed threefold: to induce calm, to develop impulsion and to help the horse find good balance under saddle. Riding across country, up and down hills, will give you your best chance to attain both of the latter results.

Lack of calm is often due to the rider himself. On leaving his stall, it is only natural for a young horse to stretch his muscles, play, cavort and even buck a bit. If, enforcing strict discipline, you stifle such gaiety, you are sure to run into trouble of two sorts: if somewhat strong-willed, the horse will fight you; if docile, he will become amorphous and turn into a plug. Since, on the other hand, you must impose your will, it is best at that early state to lunge him before you start your daily work under saddle, for about ten minutes, asking for nothing, only calming him down. Just play around with a few halts and transitions, testing and making sure of his attention which you will see increase as he relaxes. Once in the saddle, do not expect perfection either, do not ask for too much or work for any length of time without a rest. All these are precautions to prevent struggles which invariably leave traces, psychological, physical, or both.

Since at this stage of the game the development of impulsion is contingent on your ability to make yourself clear, apply the "hand without legs, legs without hand" principle. Leg action must be clear-cut, its vigor adapted to the horse's sensitivity; insist on his advancing *freely* at the very first touch. This failing, associate leg and whip. Yet keep the use of your legs down to a minimum, to pass from halt to walk or to a stronger pace, or as a reminder when the horse slows down on his own. For, if your legs are acting incessantly and without a well-defined reason, he will become enured to them and tend to let himself be carried by you. If sensitivity is to develop, rein contact must be of the slightest and supple hands must accompany the head and neck movements particular to each of the paces.

For slowdowns and halts, continue the association of your voice with your legs and hands, which will allow you to minimize the hand action to which you want to render your horse as light as to the action of your legs. No pulling, no jerking: in slowdowns and halts your shoulders should be rather more involved than your hands. At the walk prepare your horse for a halt by a definite slowdown, elbows firmly against your body but without stiffening their joints, which would result in stiffening the horse's jaw. Your thumbs are firmly closed over the reins, the other fingers keeping a soft, supple and constant contact with his mouth. To obtain the halt, keep your wrists at their place but execute a progressive and firm double movement: closing your fingers over the reins and simultaneously drawing your shoulders back the way one would in drawing oneself up tall. This sort of action exerts a "slow force" to which a horse yields easily. For a few weeks to come, continue nevertheless to use your voice in association. With the necessary preparation, an unhurried demand of this kind should produce the halt. If not, an outside opening rein will put his nose to the wall, for we must as yet avoid any hand action liable to impair impulsion.

Fig. 31. A Square Halt. An attentive horse, with impeccable head carriage, is visibly awaiting his rider's next order.

Remember in this context that your teaching can address your horse's body only via his mind, that you must make yourself understood in order to *explain*, then to *persuade*. Since any healthy horse is capable of impulsion, and good impulsion at that, it is up to you to convince him that your demands are reasonable and that, unable to elude them, it is after all less trouble to obey than to resist.

Remember also to be uncompromising with respect to the forward movement which is of capital importance. If the touch of your legs consistently fails to elicit a prompt response, if the horse remains reluctant to deliver up his impulsive forces, you must by all means make him understand the meaning of the legs and oblige him to obey them, if necessary and as a last resort, by use of rigid reins. These are an old device largely forgotten and fallen into some disrepute because often used for balky horses or rearers. But they are really very useful in making leg action more explicit to the horse and facing him with his inability to evade it. As with the use of the whip, rigid rein action following promptly upon leg action establishes the desired association in the horse's mind.

Attach two light wooden sticks (ideally a couple of spare polo mallets) to the bridle eyes, holding the opposite ends in your hands. The length of the sticks must correspond to the space between your hands and the horse's head when both are in their normal position. Thus when you extend your arms to the full the horse's neck will in turn be stretched to its own full length. This sudden weight transfer from quarters to forehand forces him to advance. The great advantage of this proceeding is domination so powerful it enforces obedience without recourse to the sort of brutality which is almost inevitable in the equally inevitable struggle of a rider armed with whip and spurs against a horse that will not go forward. Inevitable, you may be sure, because against an unwilling horse you must prevail, come what may, or give up on his training. Should someone "with the horse at heart" object to using a full bridle on a young horse, tell him (or, more likely, her) that the bit itself is not acting here. The curb chain, by acting on the lower jaw, though tight enough to prevent rubbing, causes the neck to stretch forward. Two or three days of this (walk from halt, trot from walk, speed-up, slowdown, speed-up again, rest after a few minutes, then another three or four minutes of the same) will be plenty and, believe me, not only will your horse be none the worse for it but live more happily with you ever after.

Note that you must not by any stretch of the imagination include the rigid reins as an integral part in your training method. Rare is the horse that actually requires them. Most will quite soon advance at the normal prompting of your legs, slow down and halt in obedience to your hands and turn by an opening rein. And as soon as this is the case you must go out and hack, ideally in the company of someone on a trusty lead horse. Your own will thus be less apprehensive and so, incidentally, will you. At first think of these hacks as nothing but a way to relax physically and mentally, reins long enough to let him use his neck to the utmost but short enough for light contact with his mouth. Above all, keep hands, elbows and shoulders relaxed and ever ready to follow the horse's head and neck. Do a lot of walking, on even longer reins. Riding up and down hills is excellent as long as you shun inclines so steep as to cause your horse to canter up. Don't trot for too long at a time (no more than ten minutes) and maintain an even speed. Similar rules apply to the canter which should be shorter and must on the first time out with an excitable horse follow a good long trot. Put off the occasional small jump until your "apprentice" is a bit more sure of himself and only after initiation over small riding hall fences not above three feet, on the lungeline first, then under saddle, a method succinctly outlined in the next chapter.

At this point in your progression, then, he obeys the action of both legs by going freely forward, slows down and halts in response to increased rein tension *without any backward traction on your part*, turns right or left by an opening rein, stretches his neck easily at your command without ever trying to pull on reins held separately. He is also growing increasingly acquainted with careful work on up and down grades. While it is always difficult and in fact imprudent to pinpoint a precise lapse of time, one may venture to say that this will have been achieved within four to six weeks from the first lesson under saddle. Only hereafter may we begin to make him yield to the neck rein, to the single leg which shifts the haunches, and to let him jump a few small fences, rather more for recreation than for education. The jump is after all as natural a "gait" as is the canter.

The neck rein, on the other hand, is not as natural an action to the horse as is the opening rein. So we must begin by combining both, proceeding as we did before: by a method of substitutions. To prevent misunderstandings, note that the neck rein properly applied *must not draw the head to the side of its action*. If it does, it is because the rider is pulling on this rein.

Put your horse onto a large circle, say to the left, by a light yielding of the right hand along with the leftward action of the left; but, having yielded, the right is keeping contact with the mouth, *neither decreasing nor increasing it*, chiefly producing a series of leftward and back to front wrist rotations in the direction of the horse's left ear, the rein brushing against the growth of the hair on the neck. Unless the repetition of these actions modifies the tension of the right rein, there is no reason, albeit of a mechanical nature, for the horse to incurve his neck to the right. Just at first these right-hand gestures may have to be quite repetitive, though they should never grow rapid. And, above all, there must *never* be an increase in rein tension.

Now, if you initially associate this neck rein with the opening rein, the horse will eventually understand what you are looking for. By and by you will cease to act with the opening rein a few moments before finishing your circle, will use only the neck rein and, after a while, will do so as of mid-circle, finally to do the entire circle by the neck rein alone.

Once this is carried off successfully on either hand, adjust both reins, open the fingers of one hand, for example the left, the right rein only remaining adjusted and the right hand alone asking for a change in direction to the right by an opening rein, then to the left by a neck rein, and so on. Your horse will end up by yielding to this rein effect at the mere touch on his neck. This exercise is actually far easier than it appears. The only thing to avoid is a pull which would invariably prompt a turn in the direction opposite the one intended.

Let us add that this practice will have as salutary an effect on you as on your horse, because it lets you check on what your hands are actually doing. For your own education, therefore, you may furthermore do this: stay on the track near the wall; for example, on the left hand, the right rein adjusted in the right hand but the left hanging loose. Now try to obtain a halt by repetition of light finger pressures while you straighten your upper body. If the right hand acts at its normal place, the head will turn to the right; the wall, however, will keep the horse from turning right as well as help you with your halt. Now attempt to get this halt without the help of the wall by trying to preserve, if not a straight neck, at least the travel axis: acting with the right hand to obtain the slowdown and the halt as you did before, carry this hand also slightly to the left and if necessary, upward so as to arrive, by properly combining all your actions at a halt without benefit of the wall. Repeat the very same exercise using the inside rein.

Why all this, you may ask, since no one rides with a single rein? Because it is good not only for the horse, who gets accustomed to yielding to light actions, but for yourself who are given an opportunity to refine your aids and to improve your precision.

Though criticized by some, the neck rein has a definite advantage over any other rein effect in that it acts on the neck, not on the mouth. You can carry it out, if necessary, on loose reins; that is, without any sort of opposition to the forward movement. Its execution is totally independent of the tension of the rein itself, which means that you are in a position to differentiate completely between the hand action which asks for a change of direction and that which asks for a slowdown. Acting solely on the forehand, it does not interfere with but rather promotes the forward movement.

We said above that the neck rein must not draw the head to its side of action, which is true, yet should the rider wish so, he can obtain a *placer,** for instance to the right, by increasing right rein tension and then, without changing the tension of the rein which maintains this

---

*Pronounced pla•cey. The *placer* is the position imparted to the horse's head as it is drawn slightly sideward but maintained on a strictly vertical plane. That is, the entire head is drawn aside, not only the mouth. It produces a slight crease, just enough to show the rider the orb of the horse's eye on the side of the *placer*, the other being out of sight. For example, in the left half-pass, the *placer* must be to the left.

placer to the right, ask for a change of direction to the left by a right neck rein. The essential point, to be well understood, is that this rein effect used in order to drive the forehand in a new direction has no influence whatever on the lateral *placer* of the neck. We shall discover its practical applications in studying the half-voltes haunches in and the half-turns on the haunches.

IX.
GYMNASTICS OVER POLES

If you are thinking of the dressage arena only, the jump may appear a purposeless effort to you. You would be quite mistaken. It is an excellent gymnastic exercise for the rider as much as for his horse, since it improves the balance of both. Any riding horse must be able to clear a fence willingly and adroitly without becoming a "jumping machine" and before becoming a dressage horse he must have acquired the qualities of a good "ride."

Begin in the school over variously and quite strongly colored poles on the ground. On a long rein and at the walk, go over just one of them. If your horse wants to give it a look and a sniff, let him; if he stops for further inspection, that's fine, but then click your tongue and take him over.

Now line up four poles at the proper distances for the trot, about 4 feet apart. More precisely, to prevent him from jumping across more than one at a time, you may want to place all poles at 3½ to 4 feet, then pull out the second one. Thus you are left with one, three and four, and the distance between one and three will deter your horse from wanting to take too much at one jump. At first, all these poles are placed on the track. Go over at the rising trot, sliding your hands forward along the crest. A couple of fences kept standing in the school from the start are actually a good idea, habituating the horse to a sight that consequently will no longer scare him stiff before even your first go at them.

Another time put up cross-poles not exceeding 2 feet at the center. If your previous work has been well done and your horse has so far posed no problems of his own, you can do without the lungeline. But if you feel him to be distrustful in the face of anything new, use it. If so, best place this fence rather on the track, one pole going from the top of the standard to the ground where the lungeline can pass without your hands bringing it over by a wide movement. Before you make him jump, walk alongside him toward the fence, show it to him, pat him and do so again a couple of times. Then put him at the trot onto a circle shorter in radius than the distance between you and the inside standard. When you see him at a calm but energetic trot, shift toward the fence with a click of the tongue and a wide but slow gesture of the lunging whip, but without touching him, because you want to encourage him, not urge him on. After a couple or three jumps pat him, hand him a small treat and take him back to the stables.

What if he refuses? Do not insist. Lower the poles to about 1 foot and go across beside him, two or three times; then stop for the day.

If, on the contrary, you think you can go ahead and jump him under saddle, go about it as follows: approach the fence at a walk, slow down soon enough to make him understand that you do not intend to jump. At the foot of it, halt, let him look and sniff at the poles. Then come back from a distance at the rising trot, slow down and stop as before, two or three times. Eventually return for the jump. No need to ride him strongly, just keep your legs in contact and, above all, do not forget to yield, even a little before take-off. Do not look upon this as mere hair-splitting; I have seen horses obstinately refuse a jump of less than 2 feet who responded perfectly to this procedure at the first try. Many horses are very particular about investigating what they will be about to face. Later on, once pleasant experience has taught them to trust their riders, they will pass through fire and water for them. Not so as yet.

Keep your lessons at a brisk pace; avoid monotony and its result, boredom. On the other hand, if you want to hold your horse's attention throughout, you must give him frequent, if short, rest periods.

Here is a prototype of a lesson:

Lunging work: walk, trot, walk, halt, trot, canter, on both hands, six minutes.

Immobility at the mounting: mount, get off, mount, swing your right leg over to the near side without alighting, swing it back to the offside, etcetera, two minutes.

Rising trot on the track on both hands: large circles, half-voltes, with and without neck stretching, one minute's rest at a walk on a loose rein, five minutes.

Turns at walk and rising trot: by the opening rein alone, combining opening and neck reins, by the neck rein alone, halt from the walk, immobility three seconds, one minute's rest at a walk on a loose rein, five minutes.

Rising trot with neck stretching, return to the walk, two minutes.

Canter through the trot on a circle, return to the walk through the trot, halt, immobility three seconds, rest, one minute.

Lateral mobilization of the haunches, followed each time by a departure at the trot, three minutes.

Canter on the other rein, return to the walk through the trot, halt, immobility three seconds, demand a stretch of the neck before walking on, one minute.

Rest and introduction to the very first jumps, five minutes.

We arrive at a total of thirty minutes.

To say that during any lesson the rider must know the exact goal he is pursuing is not such a truism as may appear. Inquire of a rider at work what he is after and more often than not the answer will be rather vague. Of course, a good progression must not be rigid but must keep in mind the reactions of the horse during both the present and previous lessons as well as many other considerations. Yet, any time you work on a specific movement, anything you ask for must respond to a very specific purpose. When one has nothing in particular to say, it is the better part of wisdom to hush.

X.

THE HALF-TURNS ON THE FOREHAND AND ON THE HAUNCHES

The preparatory work (that is, the lateral mobilization of the haunches) will be easier for both you and your horse if you begin it on foot and, as with all that is new, for the first time at the end of a lesson. Take a longish, above all not overly flexible whip, secure the stirrups, then place yourself at the horse's head, facing the croup, both reins in the left hand, whip in the right. Click your tongue for the walk on a circle 10 feet in diameter, whereupon your left hand asks for a slowdown, the whip acting rather far back on the flank and at the moment when the inside hind is raised. The horse will cross this hind in front of the other, do so more easily for the slowdown, which yet for the moment must never dwindle to a halt. Proceed alike with inversed aids on the other hand.

Repeat this exercise at the beginning and end of the next day's lesson, for I venture to say that the last movement of a lesson best sticks in a horse's memory. During the third and fourth lessons try to obtain the same as before, but by applying the whip closer to the place your leg would touch if you were in the saddle. Work longer on the more difficult side, without of course neglecting the other; experience has shown that, if you do, you may well end up with the originally "easy" side becoming the problem one.

After those four or five lessons on foot you ask for a similar mobility of the haunches under saddle. For a shift to the left, you take both reins at even length in the left hand, your horse on the inside track to the left. Do not hesitate to advance your left leg enough to avoid any further contact with the flank and act with your right heel by very clear-cut backward actions associated with touches of your whip; and do not lean to the right where your weight would interfere with the leftward shift of the quarters. Just as heel and whip are at the point of acting, your left hand asks for a slowdown. Beware of precipitating the movement in any way and be content with a small response. At this stage, performing a reversed half-volte is out of the question; you merely want to mobilize the haunches. During these lessons, chiefly meant to obtain lateral mobility, do not persist for too long, rather return to the exercise quite frequently in the course of your regular work. Free walk prompted by the action of both legs must follow each rotation of the haunches around the forehand.

This exercise serves a triple purpose:

1. The horse begins to flex the joints of the quarters. The engagement of the crossing hind, although artificial, is quite real.

2. In shifting his haunches, the horse is getting to know and to respect the single leg which, "resisting" later rather than "acting," will become more finely shaded. There is, however, no way to resist with a horse that has not learned to yield to this aid.

3. The rider is acquiring a means to impose a chosen direction on his mount.

Do not introduce him to half-turns on the haunches before he is at ease in half-turns on the forehand and remember that both must be performed in the forward movement. Only later will you keep him on the spot, though careful not to lose the rhythm of the pace at which you are performing. Avoid by all means the immobilization of the pivot leg, which is bound to happen if you try from the beginning to keep the horse on the spot.

Once the leg alone is able to obtain a lateral shift of the haunches, use a direct rein of opposition to reinforce your leg action. This will no doubt bring about the wrong *placer* but, on the other hand, will help your horse in yielding to the single leg. Besides, the lateral aids are clearer and more effective at the novice stage.

Obedience to the leg alone will improve if you gradually decrease the action of the inside hand to the point of becoming nil. If your horse opposes an excessive force of inertia, if the haunches keep resisting, use the spur, because it is essential to render him submissive to the single leg.

Let me insert a parenthesis on the subject of the spurs where, as here, the purpose is to increase the power of the legs when their sole action does not prevail. Be therefore sparing in their use and, whenever you must resort to them, do so by brief, sharp and, if necessary, repetitive pricks, their intensity of course commensurate with your horse's sensitivity. If your spurs stick to his flanks, he will become either blasé to them or else a nervous, ticklish tail-swisher. All the spur is indeed supposed to do is to force obedience to, but not replace, your leg. I see too many riders with their spurs in almost constant contact!

A brief remark also concerning the spur itself. The length of its neck must be determined by that of your leg. The longer your leg, the longer your spur neck if this help is to be used with a minimum shift of your leg. The shorter your leg, the shorter the neck of the spur so as to avoid accidental contact. The smooth Prince of Wales type generally suffices. If rowels are used, they must turn freely. I would also like to see you blunt their tips by rolling them against a hard surface. Whatever spurs you choose, their necks must not slant upward; rather, I should say, wear them at a slightly downward slant.

Let us return to our half-turns. Once the leg by itself easily achieves shifts of the haunches in both directions, the time has come for reversed half-voltes haunches out. Here, the hindlegs travel on a wider half-circle than that described by the forelegs. The smaller the half-circle of the forelegs and the slower the pace, the more ample will be the crossing of the hindlegs. Use of the diagonal aids will now be required; for example, left leg to shift the haunches to the right, right hand to determine the *placer* and limit the shift of the forehand. Thus with the proper *placer*, the horse will "see his haunches coming," as the expressive old French saying goes. To sum up, the aids for this movement, when left to right, should be as follows: the body weight rather to the right; the action of both hands slows the pace, the right hand moreover prompting a light *placer* to the right and regulating the lateral shift of the forehand; the left leg acts repeatedly from front to back on the flank in order to shift the haunches to the right every time the left hind is raised; the right leg at the girth maintains impulsion.

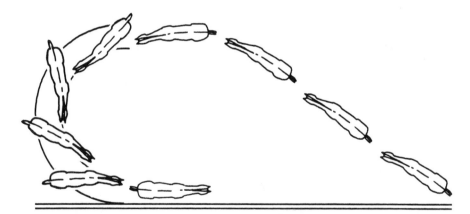

Fig. 32. Reversed Half-Volte Haunches Out. At the early stage, use of the lateral aids makes this exercise easier for the horse. Once he has learned to shift his haunches, though still with a simultaneous shift of the shoulders, the diagonal aids (in this example, right rein, left leg) will request a shift of the haunches only, the shoulders contained by the outside rein which causes him to look to the right. The previous exercise positioned the horse in a *placer* corresponding to shoulder-in; in this one his *placer* is that of half-pass.

No need to wait for these reversed half-voltes haunches out to reach perfection before you take up the half-turns on the haunches, provided the horse has learned to respond to the single leg and the neck rein, which at this stage should be the case.

In order to prepare for the half-turn on the haunches, we use the half-volte, now keeping the haunches on a smaller half-circle than the one described by the forelegs; i.e., "haunches in." Take the case of a half-volte to the left: the left hand draws the horse's head slightly to the left, while a right neck rein drives the shoulders to the left. Thus the forehand moves left while the haunches rather tend to shift right. The slightly retracted right leg must therefore keep the haunches in place. Should the horse begin to lean on it, a couple of energetic leg actions will set things right.

Toward the end of the half-circle be careful not to allow the haunches to precede the forehand: the pressure of the outside leg (the right one in the present example) must diminish and the right hand must continue to drive the forehand sideward; all the more important if you want to regain the track at the half-pass rather than merely follow the oblique on one track.

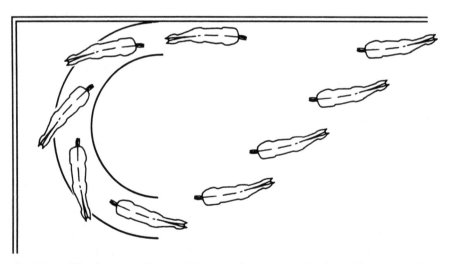

Fig. 33. Half-Volte Haunches In. This exercise prepares for the half-turns on the haunches as the previous one prepared for the half-turns on the forehand. One of them supples and lightens the haunches, the other does the same for the forehand.

If in the course of the movement the horse advances too much, it is better to lean slightly back than to act with the hands alone; for the reins will tighten with exactly even intensity, the upper body, positioned slightly behind the vertical, will burden the quarters and lighten the forehand by as much. In using your hands (left opening rein, right neck rein), rein tension must remain unchanged and correspond to whatever speed limitation you wish to impose, while the neck rein is meant to produce the lateral drive of the forehand and the opening rein is to maintain the *placer.* The slightly retracted right leg controls the shift of the haunches and the left maintains impulsion. At this stage of training the horse is not likely to understand the action of the single leg at the girth designed to maintain impulsion. It thus is necessary to associate it with a few clicks of the tongue. This, indeed, goes also for the half-turns on the shoulders.

In both sorts of half-turn it is vital to split up the action of the aids, to use at first only the active one, that is, the one shifting the haunches in the half-turn on the forehand, or shifting the forehand in the half-turn on the haunches, and for the rest to be content with slowing the pace. The supporting aids are added only after the horse yields easily to the active aids.

What we have seen shows the logic in beginning by the half-turn on the forehand, because it teaches the horse to yield to the single leg, indispensable instrument for the half-turn on the haunches. It also teaches him not just to shift his haunches but to flex the quarter joints, if you gradually increase the scope of the crossing and avoid precipitation of the steps. In other words, since the hindlegs are made to flex and advance under the mass *separately*, you take up the engagement problems one by one. Furthermore, the topline muscles are made to work in elongation. Admittedly, this movement has the drawback of burdening the forehand, while the half-turn on the haunches, on the contrary, lightens it by burdening the quarters. Hence it is up to you to find the proper dosage between both exercises for your particular horse.

The half-turns on the haunches improve the flexing of the quarter joints (coxo-femoral, stifle and hock). Combining both exercises will supple the topline, since in the present one its muscles are, on the contrary, compressed. It also prepares your horse for the rein back and the longitudinal suppling exercises and eventually leads to greater ease in the lateral shifts of the forehand.

While it is quite useful to add the half-turns on the center, where the forehand shifts to one side, the quarters to the other, the horse turning around a vertical axis passing just behind the withers, this is feasible only

Figs. 34 to 44. The Half-Pirouette at the Walk

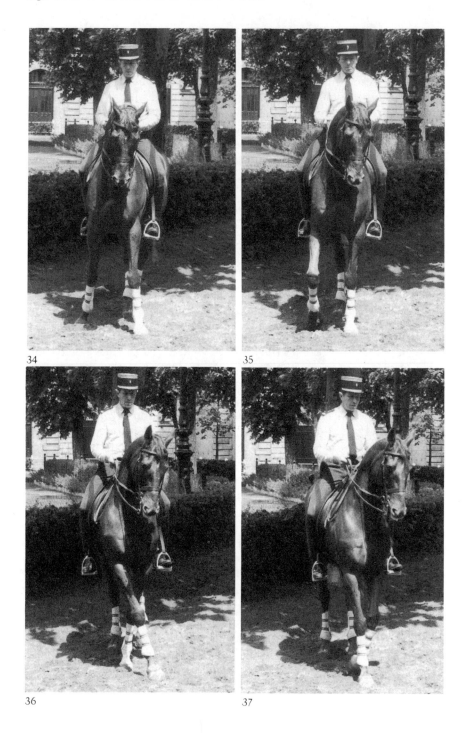

34

35

36

37

38

39

40

41

42

43

44

when the horse is already able to perform both other turns almost on the spot.

The main problem resides in performing these exercises in a state of relaxation, the only way to render them truly beneficial. Just as resistance may spring from totally different sources—being either force or weight resistances—so may stiffness have a physical or mental origin, that is, either a lack of bodily suppleness or actual, mentally-induced stiffening. Obviously, the best of suppling exercises cannot have equal results if performed by a relaxed horse or by one that is stiffening up. On the other hand, keep in mind that relaxation is contingent on the degree of speed: the slower, the more cadenced and measured the pace, the easier it is for the horse to relax, a state therefore best induced initially at the halt where the muscular system is at near rest. If one requests a light flexion at the poll, on perfectly steady hands, shoulders resisting but fingers slightly mobile, the horse will flex quite easily within a very few moments, at the same time "unlocking" his mouth.

The claim that such flexions may teach him to go behind the bit, may impede the forward movement, and so on, is not quite groundless—at least with a clumsy trainer! But then, is it really preferable to have a stiff-mouthed, unhandy horse, as rigid as an iron rod and weighing 200 pounds on the hand? However this may be, my advice addresses readers being or able to become competent trainers and who therefore understand that flexions of any sort presuppose a background of good training to the legs.

If so far I have not mentioned the departures at the canter, it was because you had as yet no classical or even semi-classical means to prompt them. Since the riding horse is by definition a galloper (as opposed to a harness horse and the trotting breeds), somewhat energetic leg action at walk or trot, combined if necessary with the whip, will almost surely prompt a departure at the canter; but on which lead? Your horse has probably a preference, which must stop short of rendering him unable to canter on either one or the other. If this should be the case, you have made a poor choice when you bought him. Normally, prompting the canter at the end of the circle just as you regain the track, you have a 90 percent chance of getting the inside lead. If not, halt, then start over and, when you get what you are looking for, do not forget to pat your horse and let him canter on for a bit. Although the canter is for now only a relaxing exercise and its utilization premature for anything else, do not let him get into the habit of always cantering on the same lead.

XI.
LATERAL AND LONGITUDINAL SUPPLING

Lateral Suppling

The work on the circle well done is the best means to improve lateral suppleness. Rarely if ever will a horse in early training follow a 25-foot circle correctly and in good balance unless your aids do more than just keep him on it. He should ideally be bent around your inside leg uniformly from head to tail, a bend obtained by the hands and the outside leg and coinciding with the curvature of the circle. When this is so, the spine's downward projection merges with the circle, the forehand does not incline inward, and the haunches won't escape outward. Obviously, the absolute continuity of the bend along the entire spine is merely apparent, since it is not equally flexible in all its parts, and one can only speak of adjusting the spine as a whole to the curve traveled by the horse.

To meet all these requirements the horse must be in good balance, supple enough to bend and able to understand your aids. Both you and he, moreover, must work with utmost precision.

The following exercises will teach the horse to bend. Consider that at liberty he will hardly turn by bending in the direction of the curve, hindlegs following in the very tracks of his forelegs. At the slow paces he will rather "turn like a ship," at the rapid ones he will bend his neck in the opposite direction. Prior to working on his haunches you must correct his tendency to let his forehand drop inward from the circle and only thereafter, and progressively, teach him to assume a more pronounced bend. It is a long, drawn-out process. Most horses are comfortable on a circle 25 feet in diameter, which does not imply that you must absolutely stick to those dimensions regardless of the reaction of your horse.

Remember now that in the proper *placer* for shoulder-in on the left rein, the horse bends left while moving to the right on two tracks. In the *placer* for counter shoulder-in, although on the right rein, the horse remains bent to the left while moving on two tracks to the right. In either case he bends in the direction opposite his lateral move, "looking whence he is coming." In the *placer* for the half-pass he bends slightly in the direction of his lateral motion, thus "looking whither he goes." To maintain an even head-to-tail bend during the work on the circle or on elements of a curve do not allow the neck, which is far more flexible than either back or loins, to bend too much. Here the supporting hand, more than just yield to let the active hand produce the inflexion, must *resist* in order to control the degree of this inflexion. One may indeed say that the supporting hand is almost more important than the active one.

Take the case of the horse which *leans into* the circle: set him onto, say, a left-hand circle about 25 feet in diameter, doing nothing to prevent him from committing the fault. But just as he starts onto an inner circle, drive him outward by a shift of both hands to the outside and a vigorous *attack* of the inside leg. These aids cease as soon as he returns onto the proper circle but resume if he repeats the fault. The hand action may take on different forms:

1. Combine a right opening rein with a left neck rein, keeping the horse bent to the left.

2. Use a left counter rein of opposition behind the withers, the intermediate rein which by itself drives the forehand and the haunches outward.

3. Or an outright shift of both wrists to the right, the left rein crossing over the neck by passing in front of the withers, the right opening rein drawing the forehand outward.

For all three exercises, remember the shoulder-in *placer* (Fig. 45).

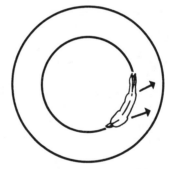

Fig. 45. Work on the Circle. Bent to the left on a left-hand circle, the horse is being driven onto a wider circle while remaining bent to the left in shoulder-in position.

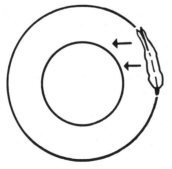

Fig. 46. Conversely, here the horse is being returned to a smaller circle in half-pass position.

You will be working at a medium trot, at least in the beginning, intent on proper impulsion. Putting the horse into free forward movement is often enough to keep him from dropping to the inside. Particularly at first, the 25-foot diameter is best for the average horse. If too wide, not only will the bend become insufficient but the horse can escape this attitude more easily, if not with his neck, then with his body. If too small, the bend will, at this stage, grow excessive and the hindlegs escape to the outside, entailing a surcharge of the forehand.

If a horse tends to widen the circle on his own, continue the very same aids, though in the opposite direction, except in case number three. Set him onto a circle, now 30 feet in diameter and drive him onto an inner circle by using (if on the left rein) a right neck rein and your right leg, with a half-pass *placer* (Fig. 46). If he pulls in order to escape your actions, change the bend which has so far been to the left, and act with a right intermediate rein to drive him to the left; *placer* of counter shoulder-in (Fig. 47).

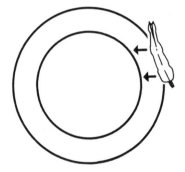

Fig. 47. The same exercise as the previous one, but now in counter-shoulder-in position.

Once your horse no longer tries to escape this circle to either side, you may go on to the following exercise. You will shift him laterally back and forth between concentric circles, alternately from wide to small, actually a sort of counter-change of hand on two tracks, the horse remaining bent to the same side. From a 25-foot diameter drive him onto a concentric circle 30 to 35 feet in diameter (shoulder-in *placer*), then return him to the original one (half-pass *placer*). While there is no expecting a true half-pass for now, you must be able to get a lateral shift in the half-pass *placer*.

Your aids are a left neck rein, a right opening rein, driving the horse to the right; vice versa in order to return him to the original circle. In either case the legs must remain at the same place: On the left rein, left leg at the girth, right leg slightly in back of its normal place. However, in driving the horse to the outside onto the wider circle, the left leg is active, the right remaining supporting, while, when returning him to the initial circle—shifting him, that is, from right to left—the right becomes active and the left supporting. The bend remains of course unchanged: to the left on a left-hand circle (Fig. 48).

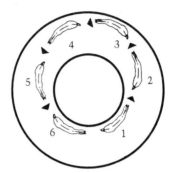

Fig. 48. Recapitulation of the exercises in figures 45 and 46.

This exercise on concentric circles is very good and to an extent improves the horse's balance, supples him, puts him "between the reins," but above all corrects his tendency to lean either inward on a curve or simply on your leg. It is also an initial step toward straightening him. Take the example of the one naturally bent to the left. You will work him on the right rein. The advantage over work on an unchanging diameter is that on a constant circle on a rein contrary to the horse's natural incurvation it is very difficult to obtain and then maintain the proper bend, while, when shifted from a smaller to a wider one, he cannot elude this bend.

Only after he has gone through this preparation and stays on either circle virtually on his own will it become possible to work effectively on one track on an unchanging diameter. Begin, as you did in lunging work, in a corner where two walls are framing the horse during some of the circle. Again, you must understand the difference between a training and a show circle. In training you should force a bit, just a little, with due regard for the horse's capabilities, but force you must if your exercise is to pay off. Unless you demand a slight daily progress you will, after a year's work, end up where you started from. So establish points of reference on the ground and, if you see the hoofprints of the hindlegs outside those of the forelegs, use your outside leg more strongly in order to place the hindlegs on a circle slightly inward of that traveled by the forelegs. If the difficulties seem excessive at the trot, take the walk and act on the circle with the same aids as you would for a half-volte haunches-in. Of course, you must not keep the horse too long on two tracks, just a few steps, back

Fig. 49. The horse is bent evenly from head to tail around the rider's left leg.

to one track, then start over. In sum, act as you would in trying to straighten a bent rod: by small, repetitive actions. While insistence on such a precise diameter may seem a bit childish, amazingly few riders have anything more than a vague sense of actual distance (Fig. 49).

Your aim is to travel at a trot of rather low and even speed on a circle 25 feet in diameter, on either one or two tracks haunches-in. While at this stage the horse is not expected to show widely separated tracks, he must be able to yield to the action of the single leg (Fig. 50).

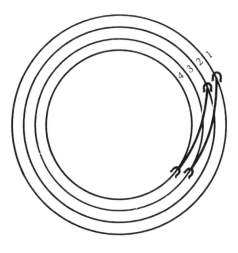

Fig. 50. On the left rein, the horse is slightly bent to the left, with both forelegs on circles 1 and 2, and the hind-legs on circles 3 and 4.

Serpentines, changing circles, changes of rein through the circle, are all excellent complementary exercises. Provided your ring is large enough, do train on non-rounded serpentines where the horse passes from a straight line onto the curve of a half-circle of an initial diameter at least equal to that of the circles he has previously been exercised on. When leaving the half-circle for the straight line of the serpentine, he must be straight and remain so in heading toward the opposite track.

Another fine exercise is to pass from one circle to another at their point of tangency, with a change of rein, provided you keep your horse from leaning inside as he goes into the new circle. Also beware of leaving him on one of these circles with any sort of regularity, or he will begin to work by rote and eventually anticipate the movement. Keep changing the number of times you let him travel each circle. What we have here is actually like a figure eight, except that he cannot foresee how often he will be doing either of the loops.

Changing reins through the circle accustoms him to passing swiftly from one inflexion to the opposite. Working, for instance, on a left-hand circle, you describe on its inside an S, the center of which corresponds to the center of the circle. Once on the diametrically opposite side, you return to the circle on the right rein. Needless to say, this circle must be wider than it was for the other exercises, because the horse must bend on a half-circle with a diameter corresponding to the radius of the circle. Thus if, in doing two half-circles forming the S, you are to preserve an inflexion corresponding to a circle 25 feet in diameter, the diameter of your large circle must now be about 50 feet (Fig. 51 for the three movements).

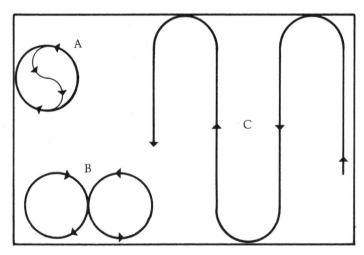

Fig. 51. A. Change of rein through the circle. B. Change of circle. C. Serpentine.

The following points are capital in all this work on circles or elements thereof:

1. Keep up a constant speed.

2. Maintain good balance by preventing the forehand from dropping to the inside.

3. Give and preserve a uniform bend.

The most commonly committed sin is an excessive bend at the neck and not enough at the body. Neck inflexion should be very slight and remain unchanged during travel on the curve. Should the horse deviate in either direction, your neck rein will set him back onto the line.

Longitudinal Suppling

Speed variations within a given pace or transitions from one to another are just about the only means we have to supple a horse longitudinally. But early on there is a lot to be said against such exercises which incite him, as yet stiff, to go onto the forehand during speed-ups and to pull during slowdowns. The rein back, of which more later, best counteracts such disadvantages. It also constitutes an excellent discipline for a horse that pulls or leans, although, if ill-applied, it is liable to ruin him physically and mentally. It therefore is a dangerous weapon if badly done or wrongly used, rendering a horse reticent, going first behind the bit and subsequently behind the legs.

Considering all this, should or should one not make use of the rein back? Most certainly, since I am not addressing riders unable to sidestep such pitfalls and who would be incapable of training a horse anyway, with or without rein back. Aside from working best and fastest toward lowering the haunches, it also best and most completely supples the lumbar region.

Be sure, though, not to begin this work before your horse moves forward keenly at the very first prompting of your legs or the click of your tongue.

Facing the horse, reins separated and held at 3 or 4 inches from the bit, we first work on foot. We raise the neck as high as his conformation allows (no hollowed back, no crushed hocks!) and, setting out from this elevation, we ask for a direct flexion, mouth relaxed, reins acting backward and slightly upward, by alternate movements of our hands. The horse will rein back one or two steps, whereupon a click of the tongue must instantly lead him forward on hands keeping a contact as light as possible but never lost.

Again, these first rein backs on foot are practiced on terminating a lesson, which allows us to reward obedience with an immediate return to the stables. Failure to yield may well be due to a slight bracing of the hindlegs caused, in turn, by an excessive length of the halt between forward and backward motion. Or else, your hands may not have worked truly upward in asking for the rein back. But if the horse persists in his refusal, fetch a whip long enough to reach his croup. Then, with your other hand steady on the rein, near the bit, the whip will prompt a slight lateral shift of the haunches and at that very instant your hand demands the rein back, straight from shoulders to haunches.

After three or four days of this, the same exercise is practiced under saddle. Except for the use of your upper body, the means are identical. Bearing down on your stirrups rather than on the saddle, elbows close to the body, lean back slightly and use your hands alternately. Remember, the hands proper must never pull back, only the fingers must close over the reins, first those of one hand, then of the other. If the horse fails to react, you shift his haunches by one, at most two lateral steps. If the rein back is crooked, increase hand action on the side of the deviation, thereby opposing that shoulder to the haunch and—as done whenever one has allowed a crooked move—*set the forehand back in front of the quarters*, rather than using your leg to place the quarters behind the forehand.

You do not need your legs to obtain the rein back, but you do need them *to prepare* your horse for it; so it is imperative for him to perceive the action of your legs in only one sense: the prompting of the forward movement, and it alone. Their use for the rein back itself—that is, urging him forward with your legs toward hands which close the door from which, so to speak, he bounces backward, conflicting aids, to say the least—teaches him fear of contact with your hand.

Prior to your actual demand, you will want to prepare your horse by some alternate hand and leg action, thus slowing him down progressively until he passes from walk to rein back by reducing the intervening halt to a minimum. The transitions from forward to backward movement and vice versa are the most valuable parts of the exercise. If then, prompting the halt, your fingers refrain from slackening but continue to maintain the same rein tension, your horse will almost surely rein back or, at least, start to do so. Admittedly, this can also be obtained by pushing him onto a resisting hand; but going against the principle of coordination of the aids and confusing the horse's mind poses a dual risk.

Each rein back must be followed instantly by a brisk forward movement. To sum up: during the rein back the legs remain close but yield; when moving on again, the hands yield without losing contact, while the legs act. This theory is very much a part of the classical French School which judges the quality of a horse's impulsion by whether or not he will move forward without the prompting of the legs as soon as the rein back aids cease to act. This is of course not feasible at all where the legs are used to obtain the rein back.

Although you begin by limiting your steps to two or three, subsequently and very gradually you must arrive at ten, twelve or fifteen rein backs, each of two to four or five steps, depending on your horse's capabilities. Never let him drop the bit or anticipate the action of your hands by backing faster than demanded. As for any other pace, what you are looking for is an ample stride, without precipitation, the horse remaining straight. And what you must avoid by all means is a hollowing of the back or stubborn locking of the hocks, automatically leading to a "crawling" rein back.

A good way to obtain the first speed-ups and slowdowns, preventing the horse from getting onto the forehand in the one, or pulling in the other case, is to put up five or six very low poles (only a few inches high and secured by insertion in wooden blocks) at distances just a little over a normal stride. Do the same a bit farther on, but spaced so as to remain somewhat below the normal stride. Whenever, as here, a horse is led to act on his own, he does so much better than he would if prompted by your aids. Instinct will make him work longitudinally the muscles of his back and loins. By and by, you associate this with the action of your aids and, eventually let these replace, on their own and entirely, the role of the poles.

Once the horse has become familiar with work on the circle, you can use still another exercise. Place your poles in a circular fashion like spokes of a wheel. The circle must be wide and the distances between the poles, as they approach the center, must vary from a normal stride at the trot to a lengthened one toward the outside and a shortened one toward the center. Since on such a very wide circle the horse's bend is minimal, one can easily pass from inside to outside and back again, asking alternately for lengthenings and shortenings of stride (Fig. 52).

Fig. 52. Exercise Poles. This arrangement allows the rider to obtain from the horse medium-length strides if passing across the center, short strides if passing across the left, and long strides if passing across the right.

In longitudinal suppling it is important not to sacrifice balance just to get a bit more lengthening and not ever to exceed, least of all in the beginning, prudent bounds in this regard. And, once more, this work should not begin at all before the horse has been suppled on the circle.

May I also remind you that lateral suppling, as previously discussed, must always precede the longitudinal kind. Dividing the difficulties of the work is the way to diminish them, since it is easier to obtain the engagement of one hindleg, then the other, than to try right away for their simultaneous engagement. The same is true in working toward the *mise en main*,* first on one side, then on the other of the circle with a *placer* of the head first to the inside, then to the outside (direct and indirect rein). It also is easier to make the spine (dorsal and lumbar vertebrae) work laterally. On the other hand, these lateral exercises tend to lessen impulsion, a tendency more or less pronounced depending on the nature of the horse and the duration of the exercises.

Alternation of lateral and longitudinal suppling lets you compensate for the drawbacks of the one by the advantages of the other. Although the lateral, let me repeat, must precede the longitudinal suppling, they are mutually complementary. In fact, improvement of the *mise en main* and of the engagement of the hindlegs on the circle will increase the quality of the speed-ups and slowdowns practiced in longitudinal suppling. And, conversely, the development of impulsion and consequently straightness through longitudinal suppling will be instrumental in increasing such impulsion in the lateral exercises (Fig. 53).

Fig. 53. Medium trot of an event horse. Note the energy of the pace.

*The combination of relaxation at the jaw and flexion at the poll.

XII.

INTRODUCTION TO THE CANTER

Departures at the Canter

Serious work at the canter at this early stage of training will in no way further the horse's education and so for now makes little sense. If you wish, let him canter a bit on the lungeline or, preferably, at liberty. Subsequently, just so he'll catch on to the idea, you may teach him to strike off, or rather fall, into the canter by the most elementary method which also happens to be the most natural.

At the rising trot *(but sitting on the inside diagonal!)*, you keep speeding up and up on the long side of the school, driving with both legs upon entering the corner. Nine times out of ten the horse will there "fall" into the canter on the inside lead. If he does not but only speeds up the trot, you press him on along the short side and into the next corner where he ought to strike off without fail. This requires no complicated lateral or diagonal aids which at this point he could not understand, just leg action, at the same place and with equal intensity, with your hands content to maintain the contact and keep the neck straight. The only difficulty you might encounter is in reaching maximum speed at the trot *just* before entering the corner. If it happens earlier and if you keep pushing, you might still get the canter, but probably on the outside lead.

The drawbacks of this method are great and various. You are liable to teach the horse to strike off through loss of balance, since he "falls" rather than "strikes off" into the canter, while the eventual goal will be to depart from the walk by rebalancing without an intervening stride at the trot and constantly to improve the walk-canter-walk transitions. The flying changes will ultimately depend on this. So doing what we are is of course not conducive to the proposed end but is only, as mentioned, a way of acquainting the horse on one or two brief occasions with its own possibilities.

Once you see him respond satisfactorily to the driving action of both legs, you may go on to true departures at the canter. This point should be reached after three or four weeks of mounted work, where we have an alternative, depending on the horse's nature and on the progress he has made so far. Whichever way you may choose, you must be sure that at liberty he canters already with equal ease on the correct lead on either rein. If he does not, you are bound for trouble with your departures now and more so later with your flying changes.

One possibility is to strike off from the walk, a slow pace granting you leisure to prepare your horse for what is to come. Your aids are more precise because you yourself are steadier, not to mention the effect of the sitting trot on the horse's back. Also, at the trot, due to its very nature, it is harder to control the haunches of a horse which is jumping from one diagonal onto the other with, each time, an intervening moment of suspension. At the four-time of the walk, the feet remain long enough on the ground to straighten the haunches, should this become necessary.

He will, even at the walk, strike off by a certain loss of balance, but a lesser one than at the trot. Once he is exercised to departing from the walk, he won't have any problem doing so from the trot; the reverse is not true. He also will be calmer at the walk and therefore more attentive. On the other hand, impulsion is of course more easily obtained at the trot, but the advantages outweigh the drawbacks.

At a brisk walk, describe a circle of an 8-meter diameter tangent to one of the short walls. A few meters before returning to the track, click your tongue as both legs intervene quite sharply and your horse will strike off on the inside lead. Two possible problems are easily overcome. The first is to accumulate enough impulsion while on the circle; the second, to obtain a strike-off just as the forefeet reach the point of tangency with the track; that is, to prepare the horse for it when still on the circle. If you only get the trot, not the canter, stop in order to discover the root of the evil, which is usually a lack of impulsion or of attention. So wake up your horse, if necessary by the whip. Or he may be a little tired; then the fault is yours. Remember that for this work he needs to be more rested than for, say, his half-turns. Or possibly, the action of your legs was not sufficiently "sharp" or you may have allowed him to lengthen his stride at the walk which should, on the contrary, be slightly shortened prior to leg action for the strike-off, much as you would compress a spring for its more foreceful release.

Prompting the canter by the lateral outside aids should be discarded, because it causes the horse to traverse himself (become crooked), while straightness is your chief problem in all canter work.

One can indeed speak of the use of regular aids for the departure on the desired lead only after the action of the single leg has become operative in shifting, in fact controlling, the haunches. In the beginning you go back to the circle and bend your horse around it, that is, around your inside leg placed slightly forward of its normal place with the outside one somewhat retracted, i.e., positioned as for the canter on the inside lead. Although the position of the legs remains the same, their action is different. Now as later, only the *intensity* of their *brief* but *sharp* intervention will vary in accordance with the horse's sensitivity and the degree of his training.

Proceeding from there, with your horse on a circle 8 meters in diameter, demand the departure by inside leg action at the girth, while the outside leg simply exerts a continuous pressure just intense enough to keep the haunches from shifting to the outside. Again, prompt the canter as the forefeet are reaching the track.

Once you obtain the strike-off with equal ease on both reins, place your horse onto a larger circle: 10, then 12 meters in diameter, eventually as large as the width of your working space will allow. Yet do keep prompting this strike-off at the moment the forefeet reach the track and while the hindfeet are still on the circle.

The next step in this progression comes when, still from the circle, you request the strike-off just a little later; that is, when the hindlegs are already on the track. Once your horse reaches the point where he almost invariably strikes off on the inside lead, you may prompt the departure shortly before reaching a corner, then by and by do so ever farther away.

There your inside hand will intervene, for this way of doing is unthinkable unless you are able to obtain a direct flexion at the poll, i.e., only with your horse in a state of relaxation. Therefore you prompt this flexion at the walk and once obtained, your inside hand demands a light lateral *placer* before you use your legs as explained above, being careful not to let the outside leg cause an excessive shift of the haunches. This outside leg action—containing, not pushing, the haunches—serves as a preparatory signal for the canter on the opposite lead.

To sum up your successive goals, remember that:

When choosing a horse, shun any animal which canters consistently on one and the same lead, on whatever rein, or which canters disunited.

Before attempting to work at the canter, be sure the horse moves freely forward at the first prompting of your legs.

Request the strike-offs departing from the walk and at this training stage do not expect a return to the walk without a transition through the trot, although its length should be held to a minimum.

Use of the circle for the departure on the inside lead keeps your horse from striking off traversed.

Associate the action of the outside leg with the strike-off prompted by the inside one.

Subsequently strike off on the straight line.

Your main hazard lies in hastily going on to the next problem before the preceding one has been completely solved. Making the horse understand the connection between the aids applied and the movement requested does require a great deal of repetition.

Once your horse backs satisfactorily, you will use the rein back alternately with the walk for your departures at the canter but be sure he strikes off directly from it without going through either walk or trot. Should this occur, stop and back another two or three steps, then strike off anew. This way you will obtain your departures by rebalancing your horse.

When working outdoors, you should persist in striking off from a circle or, for lack of space, start at the very least into a turn in the direction of the lead you wish to take.

Regarding the canter *per se*, it is wisest to remain as passive as possible in its course, to no more than accompany the movement with seat and hands. If the horse goes too fast, slow him down by associating your voice with light and repetitive hand intervention at each third beat of the canter and keeping the rhythm of the pace. If he defends himself or becomes nervous, return to the trot and wait for him to relax. If that won't do he needs more canter practice inside the school. Keep him as straight as ever you can and do not try to slow him down too much. You want to calm him, but do it at his normal speed.

Also, watch the use of your seat! A horse will often go faster than you wish simply because your seat is pushing rather than merely accompanying him. And with a frisky animal, avoid the canter on the way back to the stables.

Need one add that you must work the canter more often and longer on the problem lead?

XIII.
THE WORK ON TWO TRACKS

The time has come for explanations regarding the reins of *opposition* which are based on a mechanical *opposition* of one shoulder (the one on the side to which the neck is bent) to the haunches. Whether on one or on two tracks, they do not produce any change of direction that a proper combination of one leg with an opening or neck rein, or both, could not produce. But, although the final result is and should be the same, these reins of opposition undeniably interfere more or less with impulsion. They do so indeed to the point where they have no effect on the horse's mass unless he is in motion or else receiving sufficient leg action to impart a minimum of impulsion on which the hand can impose a direction.

You can easily test this statement on your own: at the halt, place your legs in front of the saddle flaps to make sure they cannot in any way contribute to the performance of the turn to the left that you will now be making by a left opening rein. Having bent the horse's neck to the left, he will turn left because the weight of head and neck will draw him that way, and consequently he will be taking a few forward steps to the left. If you were using a right neck rein for the very same turn, the result would be identical and for identical reasons. If you now use a direct or counter rein of opposition, the horse will either rein back while changing direction or not rein back, but neither will he turn!

Although these reins of opposition interfere with impulsion, they have a considerable advantage over the combination of your leg with opening and/or neck rein; acting as they do on the horse's entire mass, their effect can be far more finely shaded than by action on two different points of his body. Not to mention the fact that your legs will never be able to shade their effects as finely as your fingers.

Actually, in the course of your previous training you could and should have considerably lessened the risk of impairing impulsion, having given priority to its development in your work to where by now you have a horse so sensitive that a slight finger pressure on one rein will obtain the required result. So far we have not discussed the reins of opposition in depth because, the impulsion problem being the major one with most horses, it seemed wiser to abstain from their use in early training.

Let us now see how, depending on the slant of your hand action, they will be affecting the haunches or the shoulders, or both.

Choosing the example of the right *direct rein of opposition* (or 3rd effect), the right rein remains parallel to the horse's longitudinal axis, a more or less pronounced finger pressure on it increasing its tension which causes the haunches to shift to the left and thereby prompting a turn to the right. This effect may be compared to a more or less pronounced braking on the right tracks of a vehicle. Here we oppose the right shoulder to the haunches.

In executing a right *counter rein of opposition in front of the withers* (or 4th effect), the right rein makes itself felt toward the left side, following a direction passing in front of the withers. As the impulsion reaches the right hand it will inexorably shift the shoulders to the left. The direction imparted to the right rein divides the horse's motion, so to speak, in two: the forehand will turn left, the haunches, unaffected by the action, will escape to the right.

The right *counter rein of opposition passing behind the withers* (or 5th or intermediate effect) is indeed intermediate between the former two. Here the right hand makes itself felt toward the left, passing close to and rather behind the withers, somewhere between the directions of the direct and counter reins of opposition passing in front of the withers, respectively. If properly performed, this action affects shoulders and haunches equally and the entire horse will thus shift left without turning. Here again we oppose shoulders and haunches. It goes without saying that the more closely the direction of the right rein approaches that of the right direct rein of opposition, the more strongly its action will affect the haunches and less strongly the shoulders. Conversely, the more the direction approaches that of the 4th effect, the more it will affect the shoulders, the less the haunches.

It should be remembered that the supporting hand plays an important part as it limits the inflexion the active hand is giving to the neck. When, for example, this active hand performs more strongly than required, it is up to the supporting hand to resist. This results in increased rein tension amounting to a "brake" effect which, along with the change of direction or lateral shift, naturally impairs the forward movement.

Shoulder-in*

This movement has a dual application. Chiefly it is an *exercise* developing the muscle play, engaging the inside hind, therewith setting the horse on the haunches and improving his balance. It moreover works

---

*The expression "shoulder-in" signifies that one shoulder finds itself "on the inside" of the curve along which the horse is bent. In no way does it refer to the position of one or both shoulders in relation to the wall, the track or the center of the ring. One can indeed perform shoulder-in on the center line where one is neither on the right nor on the left rein and equidistant to the two long sides. Even in a wide open space, a left shoulder-in is easily distinguished from a right shoulder-in, since in the first case the horse is bent to the left, in the second, to the right. For the sake of clarity, preference should therefore be given to the French form of expression, *épaule gauche en dedans*, translated literally into *left shoulder-in*, over the current

certain muscles more intensively, particularly those of the back which is straight-forward motion have only a minimal part to ply. It also increases lateral suppleness of the entire horse more effectively and completely than any other exercise, because it combines the advantages of both the work on the straight and on the circle.

Aside from its gymnastic value, shoulder-in constitutes a powerful means of domination. While a horse can move sideways, this is by no means natural to him, nor anything he feels at ease with. In a struggle with him, therefore, the rider may even alternate such shifts to left and right in so quick a succession that it deprives the horse of any possibility to use his weight in defense. While this is for rather too spirited horses going faster than we wish, those who buck or, worse, kick at the boot are rendered materially unable to do so when put into shoulder-in, as your inside leg calls him vigorously to order. As long as the forward movement is sustained, there is indeed no way for the horse to evade your demands. So, clearly, the means by which shoulder-in is to be obtained will differ with its purpose.

As a suppling exercise it presupposes proper obedience to both legs (impulsion) and to the action of the single leg. Execution of the half-pirouette in reverse must have reached a satisfactory level of quality and your leg must be able to limit the spread of the outside hind at the instant of the outward shift which follows the crossing of the inside hind. Along the same line of reasoning, on a circle you must be able to keep the hindlegs on the same track as the forelegs.

Also keep in mind that the natural bend of the spine is usually far from even. Often the neck is inflected in two opposite directions, like an irregular "S." Trying to perform shoulder-in with such a neck is like attempting to play music on an untuned instrument. At the halt and on a loose rein, you notice indeed quite frequently a neck that is inflected along two-thirds of its length to the left and along the upper one-third to the right, or more rarely in reverse. So if you demand, let us say, a right shoulder-in, wishing to straighten the neck at its base, the upper portion, which is already bent to the right, will yield. Conversely, if you go into left shoulder-in, the base, already bent to the left, will be the one to yield. You will be using shoulder-in to correct a natural bend but, unless flexions have previously straightened the neck, all your effects will be

---

"shoulder-in to the left" which is liable to be mistaken for a reference to the horse's travel direction rather than his bend.

A similar remark applies to "haunch-in," one haunch finding itself "on the inside" of the curve along which the horse is bent. In this exercise, however, contrary to shoulder-in, the horse, bent to the left, is moving leftward.

The term "haunch-in" must not be confused with that of "haunches in," the latter referring to the position of both haunches in relation to the track or circle on which the horse is executing sidesteps.

warped. To obtain your lateral flexion at the proper place, you apply the rein on the convex side of the neck, at the spot where this convexity is most pronounced. Without the above precautions the results of shoulder-in will remain disappointing.

The question of whether this exercise should be performed on three or four tracks is a pseudo-problem created not so long ago by the F.E.I. and it requires a clear statement of the actual facts. In the eighteenth century, La Guérinière (that is, the French School) invented and used shoulder-in as a training exercise (albeit on four tracks), and not by any stretch of the imagination as part of equestrian displays. It is the F.E.I.'s prerogative to include this movement in its tests and even to stipulate, as happened lately, that it be performed on three tracks. On the other hand, it should fastidiously refrain from the misleading appelation "shoulder-in" rather than "half-shoulder-in" as La Guérinière very precisely and completely defined this form of the movement in Elémens de Cavalerie, a work not to be confused with Ecole de Cavalerie but, alas, familiar only to specialists (Fig. 54).

Demi-epaule en dedans (half-shoulder-in)
according to La Guérinière's instructions; quote:
"Put him in half-shoulder-in; that is, bent to the side to which he moves, he must place his outside forefoot on the line of the inside hind."
Track 1: left forefoot
Track 2: right diagonal
Track 3: right hind

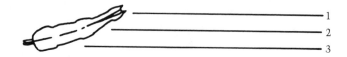

Fig. 54. Half-Shoulder-In

Historically, therefore, the F.E.I. is wrong, but worse is to come: ignorant or disingenuous, that assembly sitting in majesty has thrown a mantle of silence over the matter so that the average rider is now left to imagine that the true shoulder-in is performed on three tracks. More royalist than royalty itself, there are among those who should know better a few avid champions of fantasy theories who accuse La Guérinière's shoulder-in of causing a horse to go behind the bit, overbend and other deadly sins. The reigning body would therefore do well to emerge from its mutism and clarify its point of view for the benefit of its confused subjects.

Never mind, La Guérinière, Generals L'Hotte and Decarpentry for the French School, Colonels Podhasky and Seunig for the Germanic School, to name just a few of the most authoritative equestrian sources, prescribe shoulder-in as performed on four tracks. Half-shoulder-in, because it causes but a minimum bend, does obviously find its proper place in their work, as in ours. As in all suppling exercises, a small effort is demanded to start with, increasing as progress allows from half-shoulder-in to shoulder-in.

You start into this exercise from a basic circle whose radius will determine the horse's bend. You bend your horse on the circle (10 meters in diameter), going around as often as necessary to obtain the correct incurvation and the proper impulsion. This achieved, you return to the track where you demand a few steps of shoulder-in along the wall. This demand must coincide with the instant when, hindlegs still on the track, the forelegs are already on the base-circle (Fig. 55). A very few steps, then finish the circle *moving on one track*, which restores the impulsion without losing the bend and leaving the horse ready for another few steps at shoulder-in. As in all cases, modest but frequent demands achieve the best results.

left shoulder in starting from the circle.

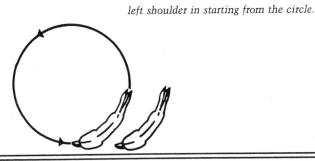

Fig. 55. Left Shoulder-In Starting From the Circle

Do we begin at walk or trot? Preferably at the trot, where impulsion is more readily sustained, even, I daresay, at the rising trot. Since, however, in skipping from one diagonal onto the other, the horse evades a goodly part of the crossing effort, effective suppling will eventually require concentration on the walk.

Again, to safeguard impulsion, the bend should at first be slight and the crossing effort minimal, but by and by, with improving performance, you

Fig. 56. Left Shoulder-In on the Center Line. Note the crossing of the hindlegs.

must increase the bend. Do not insist upon the lateral movement for any length of time and invariably follow it up with a good extension of the pace.

Your aids for a left shoulder-in might be a left intermediate rein which will shift shoulders and haunches in equal measure to the right and impart a leftward bend. Here your legs play but a single, though capital part: they create and maintain the impulsion.

Another, far more delicate procedure is the following (example again *left* shoulder-in): Your left rein has a dual role in prompting the bend to the left and driving the shoulders to the right (neck rein). The right (supporting) hand limits the bend of the neck but also guides, if necessary by an opening effect to the right, the shoulders to the right. The left leg, around which the horse is bent, is driving him forward and to the right; the right leg, slightly in back of its normal place, not only helps the bend but prevents the haunches from escaping to the right (Fig. 56).

Fig. 57. The Extended Trot. The horse's frame has lengthened in accord with the lengthening of the pace. Impulsion and engagement (note the right hind) endow the pace with fulsome energy, yet without impairing balance. The horse is working in muscular harmony.

Avoid two common faults. Instead of crescent-shaped, the horse may come to be incurved like a bishop's crozier; that is, rather than evenly bent from poll to tail as he should be, he is more strongly bent in the neck than along the rest of his body. The second fault is to permit the head, which must remain at the vertical, to tilt sideways

Haunch-in

This exercise is best and most concisely defined as the exact opposite of shoulder-in. If the horse is bent, for example, to the left, he will move left, instead of right as he would in left shoulder-in. Also, in shoulder-in the greatest crossing effort falls to the forelegs, in haunch-in it falls to the hindlegs. Both exercises are comparable in difficulty to execution of the half-pirouette in reverse with either direct or counter-*placer*. With a counter-*placer* it is harder to perform; this is likewise true for haunch-in which poses greater initial problems than shoulder-in. Yet both shoulder-in and the half-pirouette in reverse with a counter-*placer*—where, as the picturesque saying goes, "the horse sees its haunches coming"—have prepared him for haunch-in. As usual, be for now content with just a few lateral steps but demanding as to their quality. The position of the horse should not exceed an angle of 20 degrees or so in relation to the wall.

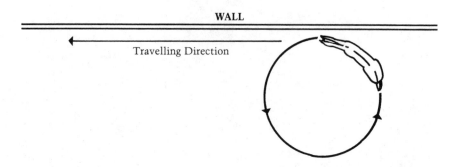

Fig. 58. Left Haunch-In. Once more, as in figure 55 for shoulder-in, the constraints of space versus visibility cause this sketch to show an excessive curvation of the horse.

Setting out from a sufficiently large circle in order to limit the crossing effort, you now proceed as you did for shoulder-in. Yet in this instance the horse will be driven laterally by the outside leg and rein at the moment when, at circle's end, the forelegs reach the track. In shoulder-in, on the contrary, it was (if you remember) at the moment when the hindlegs left the track that your inside leg and rein prompted the crossing.

Within one and the same bend it is the travel direction that determines which fore or hind leg assumes the heaviest task. Although, for example, in both left shoulder-in and left haunch-in the horse is bent to the left, in the former he travels to the right, in the latter to the left. In this leftward bend, the legs of the left lateral are nearer each other than those of the right. This places the left hind slightly forward of the right one, while the reverse is true regarding the forelegs, the left finding itself slightly behind the right. In shoulder-in, easy to see, the left foreleg, slightly behind the right, will have to make a greater crossing effort than the left hind placed by the general bend slightly forward of the right. In haunch-in the picture is exactly reversed, the right hind bearing the brunt of the crossing effort. This lets you work at will not just one side more than the other but, even on the same side, single out a specific fore or hind, depending on your choice of either shoulder-in or haunch-in.

To continue with the example of the horse bent to the left: concentrate your particular attention on the left hind. In shoulder-in the haunches must not skid to the right; your right leg must control, albeit limit, the crossing to make sure that this hindleg does not fail also to advance. In haunch-in your left leg must assure the engagement of the left hind in order to keep it from escaping to the left. This very risk requires special care in preserving both impulsion and speed within a given pace, increasing the crossing only gradually as the free forward movement allows. These two exercises have now prepared the horse for the half-pass.

Half-pass

By all classical canons the horse must remain straight, with just a slight lateral *placer,* which is sufficient when the rider can see the horse's eyeball on that side.

Begin with half-voltes and, on reaching the end of the half-circle as you enter the oblique on the way back to the track (that is, with your horse's forehand nearer the track than his haunches), you will be driving him on with combined outside hand and leg action. These are the determining aids, while the inside hand uses an opening effect to draw his head in the travel direction. You might say that the half-pass combines alternately the aids of the half-turns on the forehand and on the haunches. This procedure sets an automatic limit to the number of steps; the wall in front of you makes it easy to check your horse's exact position and the approach of the track, which always attracts a horse, helps to maintain his impulsion. Following three or four steps at the half-pass you lengthen stride to regain whatever impulsion may after all have been lost.

While the half-pass *head to the wall* has the definite advantage of keeping the horse neatly on his tracks, it forcibly somewhat impairs the forward movement. If the angle with respect to the wall is very small (20 degrees) the risk is negligible, but so is the above-mentioned advantage! In this early work you will therefore give preference to *tail to the wall* which, thanks to your past practice of shoulder-in, your horse can maintain for several steps. Though it is a bit more difficult in that he may tend to leave the track, it allows you, should impulsion flag, to stop the half-pass at any moment and drive him straight ahead. What is more, not now facing a wall, he will be less likely to slow down. Moreover, you are given full assurance of his submissiveness to the aids, since they alone now control position, direction and speed.

Your aids for the half-pass from right to left are as follows: the dominating (active) ones are the right neck rein driving the forehand to the left and the right leg slightly in back of its normal place driving the haunches left and forward. A left opening rein imparts the *placer* to the left, while simultaneously drawing the forehand toward the left. The left

Fig. 59. The Half-Pass. A nice combination of forward movement and leg cross-ing.

leg acting at the girth maintains impulsion. If you weigh slightly more on your left stirrup than on the right, you will accompany your horse's left-ward shift but be careful to be neither ahead nor behind his movement and not to tilt your upper body, careful also to keep the effect of the inside rein (the left in our example) from acting on the haunches and thereby im-peding their leftward shift.

To improve your half-pass, perform a few steps of it from the long side of the ring toward the center. Thus, finding yourself on the left rein, you wait until you have passed the corner leading onto one of the long sides and there ask for three or four steps at the half-pass to the left, carefully shifting the forehand first. Then straighten your horse to be strictly parallel to the long side and for a few steps, straight and on one track, lengthen the stride. By another few steps at the half-pass you either return to the track or, on the contrary, half-pass in the same direction as before. Remember that varying your movements is of the essence if you want to keep your horse from anticipating them!

All such exercises are principally done at the trot but with a horse that tenses up in body or mouth (usually both) you should return to the walk for two or three steps at the half-pass, then only continue the movement at the trot. Whether you use walk or trot, remember the advantages of either without forgetting their respective drawbacks in picking the pace most apt to overcome the current difficulty. You might even avail yourself of the rising trot, sitting on the diagonal corresponding to your half-pass direction: left diagonal for the half-pass from right to left. While you are less close to your horse, you are steadier at the rising trot; but prior to choosing your diagonal you will do well to try both, for there are exceptions to the rule.

Throughout this period avoid the half-pass at the canter where, at any rate, the crossing effort is almost nil. Nothing to gain by it and much to lose, because it may encourage your horse to traverse himself even more than is natural at the canter. It should not be attempted before he is quite straight at that pace and half-passes at both walk and trot with equal ease on either rein. Once this has been achieved, the half-pass at the canter is unlikely to pose any problems.

The half-pass on the circle, with haunches out, haunches in

This movement is designed for the improvement of the half-pass rather than for "show." If your purpose is to work specifically on the left hind, you place the horse on a left-hand circle, haunches out. Since the hindlegs travel a larger circle than the forelegs, they will have to strain more, most particularly the left hind. Placed, on the contrary, haunches in, one of the forelegs will bear the brunt of the effort. The latter exercise is useful in preparing the half-pirouette and, later, the full pirouette at the walk and at the canter. In order to prevent alteration of the pace in both half- and full pirouettes, the pivot leg must remain mobile. Your half-pass on the circle with haunches in is instrumental to that end, because it causes the hindlegs to describe a very small circle, just large enough to oblige them to move on at each step of the pace, in other words, to remain active. The dimension of the inner circle (described by the hindlegs) is gradually reduced, as impulsion, suppleness and, particularly, the flexibility of the hindlegs allow until you reach the point where you can keep the inside hind (the pivot leg) on the spot, yet mobile, that is, maintaining the pace unadulterated. This is indeed the only rational way to habituate a horse to executing correct pirouettes, which are generally performed at the walk or the canter. It can be done at the trot, provided the horse knows how to piaffe!

Counter-changes of hand on two tracks

Here even more than elsewhere, the soundest principle is to tell your horse what is expected, then let him do. Initially, you keep him straight for three or four steps between shifts to give him time to change his direction: if you begin a counter-change of hand on two tracks by three or four steps of half-pass to the left, you will straighten your horse and take him straight ahead for another three or four steps before going into the half-pass to the right. This way your aids will work neatly, without precipitation, and you give your horse a chance to understand.

Begin at the walk, which being slower makes it easier to change your half-pass direction. Little by little you reduce the intermediary steps and your horse, now knowing what is expected, will on his own get ready to change direction when the signal comes. Never mind, as long as it materializes only at your command, that this is clearly a kind of anticipation. For a perfect counter-change of hand, the horse would have to be perfectly parallel to the long sides of the arena, so great a precision as to be virtually unfeasible, because for a couple of inches at each step it would cause the haunches to precede the shoulders, which, on the contrary, should precede them in the lateral shift. But if, about to change the half-pass direction, you give him his new *placer* and the new bend of his body, the shoulders will continue to shift ahead of the haunches (Fig. 60).

In conclusion, let me remind you of what is most important to recall:

1. Not the crossing, but sustained impulsion and the proper engagement of the inside hind are your major problems.

2. The lateral shift of the shoulders must consistently precede the shift of the haunches.

3. Be content with just a few consecutive lateral steps, mindful to keep the horse relaxed.

4. For both shoulder-in and haunch-in, depart initially from a circle large enough to produce only a slight bend.

Fig. 60. The Half-Pass. The late Col. J.A. Brau on his Olympic Horse *Quai des Brumes*. One of France's top polo players in his younger years, he eventually and successfully took up dressage. Rare indeed is the sight of a horse crossing his legs to such a degree. *Courtesy Col. J.A. Brau.*

XIV.
CANTER, COUNTER-CANTER AND FLYING CHANGES OF LEG

The departures at the canter must be constantly improved. Since every horse is more at ease on one lead than on the other, we have—whether in or out of doors—quite consistently cantered on the less comfortable one. So now that problem has been solved, as have all other basic ones by work on strike-offs on the circle, and the time has come to strive for straightness and lightness at this pace, for instant departures, better balance and the *mise en main*.

Your departures will be effected mostly from the rein back and the walk, and for both straightness and better balance you will make use of the counter-canter. But remember throughout that none of it will pay off unless your horse is relaxed. If he is somewhat cold to the leg, prompt the departure by the leg alone; if he is rather sensitive, do so by the hands which produce calmer, thus smoother departures. This is true also regarding the flying changes of leg. Associating the action of the inside hand, which gives the *placer* (left hand for the left canter), with the propulsive aid, which determines the canter on a given lead (inside or outside leg), you will soon obtain the departure by the rein alone.

Note that there is no general agreement regarding the horse's rectitude at the canter. He is considered to be straight when, on one track, the spine-to-ground projection merges with the line of travel; meaning that he is *straight* from head to tail on a *straight line* and *bent* on a *curve* in strict conformity with the latter's bend. And yet, one does wish to have a slight *placer* of the head at departure and even to see it maintained throughout the canter: *placer* to the left for the left, to the right for the right canter. Straightness should in principle be absolute, without any lateral *placer*; in practice this is virtually impossible, except with a very highly trained horse.

To make ourselves clear to our mount at this stage of training, anyway, requires such a light inflexion. So, departing on the left lead, for example, the slight *placer* to the left will inflect the neck to the left, render it concave there and convex on the right. On a relaxed and properly suppled horse this will produce a weight shift from left to right, burdening the right as it relieves the left.

But what about the horse counter-cantering on the circle, where his inflexion no longer corresponds to the line of travel, quite the contrary indeed, since his *placer* continues to correspond to his lead? It supposedly must be so because the horse cannot be bent to the left on a left-hand circle while cantering on the right lead. This gives quite naturally rise to the next question: when changing lead at every fourth stride on a left circle, what must be his bend? And at every second stride? Different people have attempted to deal with this Gordian knot in different ways, none satisfactorily which is the reason in all likelihood why the F.E.I. has excluded the counter-canter on the circle from its tests.

The Counter-Canter

To acquaint the horse with this movement progressively, increasing the difficulties only gradually, and without actually constraining him to counter-canter, you will choose a space of sufficient size not to *impose* the changes of direction by reason of its limitations. You start with the lead he originally preferred and are careful to keep your hands and legs where they have acted in determining the strike-off when commencing your change in the direction opposite as you follow a wide curve, without intensifying your aids beyond more maintenance of speed. Should the pace grow irregular, rechange direction to return to the true canter. A bit farther on, once more counter-canter, but if your horse changes lead or, as happens more frequently, becomes disunited, stop everything, rein back a few steps and start over on the same lead as before the fault occurred. Needless to say, you must not punish him for changing lead or disuniting; he would remember it later when you will be trying to teach him the flying change of leg. As he is gaining in ease on wide curves, you gradually narrow these, changing direction by the rein opposite his lead: at the left canter, use the right (direct) rein on turning right and the right (neck) rein for a turn to the left.

Although the counter-canter may be taught relatively early in your progression, it should be done only after full satisfaction with the *mise en main* at the canter, i.e., *ramener* complete with relaxation at the jaw. Once more, remember that the work at the counter-canter is valid only with a relaxed horse.

I should here open a parenthesis concerning shoulder-in at the canter. Some condemn, others recommend it. I indeed believe that, provided you have enough impulsion, shoulder-in works the equine skeleton most effectively at the walk. Although impulsion poses no real problem at the trot, the horse's skipping from one diagonal onto the other lets him evade the true crossing and bending efforts. However this may be, at both paces shoulder-in is a general suppling exercise, which cannot be said for it when performed at the canter, except perhaps for correcting a natural bend aggravating that caused by the pace *per se*.

The above may require some explanation. Horses are congenitally bent more or less to one side and the asymmetry of the canter causes their haunches to deviate slightly toward that of the lead. When that lead is the left, the tendency of a horse naturally bent to the left will be aggravated by the cumulation of natural and canter incurvation. But when the same horse canters on the right lead, the two different bends just about cancel each other out.

The very fact, then, that the horse's quarters will naturally bear off at the canter counsels against early practice of the half-pass at this pace. Faced as you would be with a dual straightening problem of dual origin, avoid it, unless your work on the circle at walk and trot and at shoulder-in has rendered your horse by now virtually straight at the canter. But if you feel able to maintain your horse very nearly straight and to prevent any lateral shift, we see no objection to a very light shoulder-in at the canter. In such a really minimal shoulder-in position, your horse's haunches are framed between inside rein and outside leg, aside from rendering the engagement of the inside hind more effortless. To keep the quarters from bearing off during your canter on the track, orient the forehand slightly toward the inside to produce a rectilinear position. Consider that the space between the shoulders is less wide than between the haunches, so if you were to place the outside shoulder as close to the wall as the outside haunch, your horse, positioned on a slight oblique in relation to the track, would indeed be somewhat crooked (Figs. 61 and 62).

Fig. 61. Straightness at the Canter. The haunches being by nature wider than the shoulders, in order to keep the horse straight the rider must draw the forehand slightly toward the center as shown here.

Fig. 62. Or the horse will appear as here, slightly traversed to an onlooker facing the rider strictly from the front, the left hind not quite aligned with the left fore.

Once all his balance problems have been solved and he is able to perform an unperturbed canter, whether turning right or left, whether at true or counter-canter, at an unvarying speed on *elements* of relatively wide circles, you may begin exercise at the counter-canter on the actual *circle:* if your horse is naturally bent to the left, you counter-canter on the right lead on the left rein, without totally neglecting the reverse exercise.

In the course of this slow progression you must reach the point where your horse, whether on or off the track, will strike off instantaneously from the walk on the desired lead. This requires patience, perservance and repetition, which must not, however, border on routine. As with the human trainee, only repetition will make an indelible imprint on the horse's memory and therewith create the reflex reaction which equates instant response; alas, the repetition-memory process is effective for wise and unwise lessons alike. There is no wisdom in the best of lessons unless the horse is given a chance to carry out what he is being taught and this "chance" translates into "balance, relaxation and impulsion."

Rare are, alas, the riders able to detect resistance before it actually materializes, so all I ask of you for now is to stop immediately upon its physical appearance in the form of either a wrong movement or one undertaken at the horse's own initiative. When, on the contrary, he performs at your bidding, do not interrupt the movement with undue haste. Whatever the resistance you are obliged to oppose, do so with calm aids carefully adjusted to your horse's character. A good rider never reacts in anger but punishes his horse, in case of need, as would a sort of "superior power." Although, on occasion, your fingers must shut energetically, much as an iron curtain might descend, a split second later they must already have softened to the minimum contact required.

If you have been working along these lines, you are now able to obtain the canter on the lead of your choice, from the walk, on the center line, by the diagonal aids (left rein, right leg for the left canter), and with a straight horse, then to return (somewhat more of a problem) directly to the walk without provoking a defense, all of it by mere indications of your aids devoid of any forceful action. Failure to return calmly to the walk is a symptom of still defective submissiveness to your aids, a problem often due to lack of either balance or engagement, or both. If so, momentarily give up this exercise and concentrate on whatever is likely to improve your horse's balance and the flexibility of his quarters, whether at the walk or at the trot.

Flying Changes of Leg

Sure of your smooth departures and returns to the walk, you now may broach the subject of the flying changes. Again, you have a choice of procedures.

1. Place your horse on the rein corresponding to his preferred lead (say, the left) on a circle just wide enough to maintain the counter-canter. Make him depart on the outside lead and, after a few strides, change from right to left canter aids, commanding a strike-off on the left. This action should in principle take place at the end of the second canter time, since the duration of the third will allow for your signal to reach the horse's brain and for his brain, in turn, to signal the change to his legs which, then, will perform it during the time of suspension. Note that relaxation and proper balance are more important here than ever. For a smooth change, do not let him slow down too much and do not set him excessively on the haunches. This is really the most classical way.

2. You also might perform a half-volte sufficiently distant from a corner to be able to return to the track at a place slightly before the same corner, there to demand the flying change.

3. Or you may demand the flying change at the end of a change of rein on the diagonal, i.e., just as you approach the corner.

4. Else, canter on the inside lead, that is, on the correct one, and command the change on a straight line. Illogical as it may seem, this procedure is designed to assure rectitude during the change, which is of course valid only in the school, where the wall provides a barrier.

5. Still another choice is the serpentine where the change is commanded at the very top of a loop tightened, if necessary, to enforce the change. I do not advocate this manner, because the abrupt narrowing of the second part of the loop is liable to set your horse on the forehand and therewith cause a disunited canter.

If you are working on your own and, for lack of a trained horse, have never felt a flying change of leg under your seat, you might consider another, although far from classical and hardly commendable way. You jump a three-foot upright fence, set up at the center and built to be taken in either direction, a couple or three times consistently at the trot; then, still at the trot, you take it at an oblique which you will gradually increase. By the time the horse does well on this approach, jumps the fence easily and across its very center, you pass on to the canter. Ride a figure eight, its central point corresponding to the fence. During the jump you prepare your horse for a turn as near to the point of landing as possible where the change of direction will cause him to change lead on his own. The great drawback is of course that you teach him to change at his own sweet will rather than at the prompting of your aids. So let us call it, if not a gimmick, a last resort.

In reality, before you can attempt to teach your horse the flying change of leg the movement must have "entered" your own body. They may tell you that it is all a matter of proper mechanics and that, to obtain a flying change of leg, you must cease the aids having determined the initial canter and demand a new strike-off on the other lead; that is, restart from one canter into the opposite. Even assuming that you know the appropriate canter time for the action, you will find this theory practically worthless. Recalling all you would have to do in that split second would paralyze your aids, keep you from going with your horse's motion, and render the entire movement very abrupt.

If, let us assume, all has gone well so far and your flying changes are now performed with ease from outside to inside and vice versa, the time has come to go beyond the single ones. We were saying "outside to inside" rather than "counter to true canter," because on a straight line there really is no such thing, except in the school or dressage arena where the rider in his own mind anticipates the passing of an approaching corner and where, alone, one may make this distinction.

From the walk, demand five strides at the canter, then return to the walk. Demand another five on the other lead and again return to the walk. Although working both sides, change your sequences so as not to fall into routine. If these departures and returns to the walk are obtained calmly and without confusion, the horse is ready for the flying change at every sixth stride. While it all sounds easy on paper, in practice it is not quite the same, particularly because in progressing to more frequent changes the transitional strides decrease until, at every stride, you actually face something like a pace in its own right.

It may be said that here the rider's aids are constantly acting on the opposite side to the ongoing lead. To make things a bit easier for your horse and yourself, do strike off on a circle, on the inside lead, then command a change to the outside, followed immediately by the opposite command, thus returning to the initial canter. Make certain your aids work with utmost precision and here, as with all flying changes (whether at every other, third, or fourth stride), proceed slowly, do not ask for too many at a time, but go back to them frequently and give all your care and attention to their quality: straightness, smoothness and ampleness.

Without minimizing the problems involved, let us demystify the flying changes: while they do not "happen by themselves," a horse well prepared throughout the previous progression should take to them as to something that "comes natural" (Figs. 63-65).

Fig. 63. The Flying Change of Leg. At the time of suspension, the horse starts to change lead from left to right.

Fig. 64. The horse is at the first beat of the canter to the right, just after the change. ▼

Fig. 65. ▲
The first beat of the canter to the right during a sequence of changes at every stride, the rider's right leg already prompting one more change.

XV.
PIROUETTES

The pirouette, a complete circle described by the forelegs, one hind serving as a pivot, is generally executed at the canter. Half-pirouettes, albeit in the F.E.I. tests, are performed at the walk, but nothing prevents one from doing a full pirouette at the walk, or at the trot which then actually turns into a piaffe, or even a double pirouette at the canter.

In any case, before the work on pirouettes can begin, the horse must be taught to perform half-pirouettes at the walk, as well as to canter slowly enough to make five or six strides causing little if any advance. This, needless to say, presupposes a highly trained horse: well-balanced, flexible and of truly superior impulsion. Although mechanically simple, both pirouette and half-pirouette, if correctly performed, pertain therefore to the *haute école*.

Beginning by half-pirouettes in reverse (or half-turns on the forehand, which is the same thing), the horse's haunches will be rendered light, mobile and as responsive to the single leg, which controls their direction, as to both legs, which prompt the forward movement. As usual, the work proceeds by stages.

Your first goal is the lateral mobility of the haunches. So, setting out from a slowed-down walk, you act with one leg which, along with a direct rein of opposition on the same side to reinforce the effect, will shift the haunches in the opposite direction. By these lateral aids—that is, in no danger of giving conflicting signals—you make your intention extremely clear to your horse. Unfortunately, these aids cannot control his forehand which is bound to shift, if ever so slightly, in the same direction.

This must be corrected at the following stage and can be done only by teaching the horse now to shift his haunches by the diagonal aids. It will enable you to block the movement of the forehand by applying your left rein to the neck while your right leg drives the haunches to the left. The use of this rein is, however, rather a delicate matter, because its action must be strong enough to restrain the shoulders, but not so strong as to drive them in the opposite direction.

The work described is done on a reversed half-volte; as the name indicates, a half-volte traveled in reverse. Rather than starting by a half-circle and returning to the track by an oblique, leave the track by an oblique and return to the track by a half-circle. This said, your exercise consists of shifting the haunches onto an outside track to make the horse travel your half-circle on two tracks, forelegs on the inside, hindlegs on the outside track.

At this point you must give some thought to making the forehand shift laterally and with equal ease. Since here (now turning around the quarters) you will be using the haunches as a pivot, where they must be prevented from shifting, you now realize how essential it has been to begin by the half-pirouettes in reverse.

At present use the half-volte, your outside leg keeping the hindlegs on an inside track during the half-circle, the forelegs following the outside track. Again, the horse will be moving on two tracks, but now the forelegs on the outside, the hindlegs on the inside one. The shoulders are moved sideways to, say, the left by a right neck rein, seconded by a left opening rein which causes the horse to look to the left. Your right leg keeps the haunches on the inside track, the left leg, acting at the girth, maintains the impulsion.

Both exercises (haunches turning around the forehand, and vice versa) must be performed with ease, breaking neither the walk nor its rhythm. The better the horse's balance and the more relaxed he remains throughout the movement, the better your half-pirouette will be.

You now begin to work on a full circle, haunches in, varying and eventually reducing its size to where its radius equals the length of your horse. At this point, the hindleg serving as a pivot will remain at the center of the circle described. Your major problem, rather than to keep this pivot leg in place, is not to lose the regularity of the walk. Only with time will sufficient flexibility of joints, along with improved impulsion, enable a now properly balanced horse to maintain his pivot leg on the spot without disrupting the four-time of the pace. So keep in mind that only a slow progression will lead to a true half-pirouette at the walk.

While following this particular progression, however, you have also been busy teaching your horse to cadence his canter which, with increasingly flexible joints, he now performs almost on the spot. A successful combination of both movements equals, in fact, a pirouette at the canter. Here is how to go about it.

While performing a pirouette at the walk, you prompt a departure into the canter for only one or two strides, continuing your pirouette at the walk but prompting another departure at the canter before the end. This teaches the horse to shift his forehand sideway during the canter, while the limited number of strides (one or two) robs him of any chance to quit the circle. But by the time you increase their number, be careful to keep all four feet moving, without precipitation of beats and in the strictest *mise en main.*

In the final preparatory exercise, the half-pass at the canter croup to the wall, you travel on an inside track at a horse's length from the wall. As you reach the end of the side you are on, ask your horse to do a half-pirouette without breaking the canter. Framed by the corner formed by the two walls, you will hardly need your reins to keep him at the half-pirouette. Once this works perfectly, you do the same at increasing distances from the wall, until you reach the point of performing the movement with none but your own aids at the center of the school.

The aids for the complete pirouette at the canter do not differ from those for the pirouette at the walk. That is, for a pirouette to the left: left opening rein to place head and neck; right neck rein to drive the forehand to the left; the left leg, a bit more forward than ordinarily, the horse slightly bent around it, maintains (and this is of the essence!) the impulsion; the right leg, on the contrary somewhat retracted, restrains the haunches. Your horse's head carriage and your leg *position* are basically as they would be at the normal canter, but in the pirouette your leg *action* takes on unprecedented importance as the agent which maintains the all-important impulsion.

Let me just add that people may have spoken to you of a difference between half-pirouettes and half-turns on the haunches or half-pirouettes in reverse and half-turns on the forehand. There is, as has been seen, none whatsoever, except that half-pirouettes have been included in dressage tests and pirouettes in reverse are used as home exercises—and that is all there is to it.

Finally, I would like to offer a helping hand to those who, in their studies of classical equitation such as this, like to go back to the sources, namely the works of the eighteenth century, where they sometimes happen onto confusing terms. In the context at hand, let me mention that the use made by La Guérinière and his contemporaries of such unfamiliar and often archaic terms as voltes in opposition to something called "reversed voltes" is due to a fact that at the time the volte was either a circle *(volte à l'ancienne)* or else a square, where the horse moved on two tracks, never on one! When done head to the outside, haunches to the inside, it was a "volte;" head to the inside, haunches to the outside, it was a "reversed volte." This is just one example among many (Figs. 66-68).

Figs. 66 & 67. The Pirouette at the Canter. This clearly shows the dissociation of the diagonal on the ground during the second beat of the canter, as caused in all pirouettes by the maximal slowdown of the pace.

Fig. 68. Note the very pronounced engagement of the hindlegs.

XVI.
Passage and Piaffe

The *passage* is a trot of shorter strides than those of the collected trot, loftier too, with longer times of suspension. The *piaffe* is but passage performed on the spot. Both airs derive their value as much if not more from the regularity and slowness of their rhythm as from the elevation of their beats. Setting out to slow the collected trot, one may begin by the passage, or begin by the piaffe from which will then flow the passage, though it is wisest to develop both simultaneously: more conducive to those smooth transitions from one to the other and in reverse. Therein, if performed without alteration of rhythm and regularity, lies the art and the difficulty. If the horse is confirmed in its piaffe before being introduced to the passage, the piaffe-passage transition will pass through a sort of hiatus, though the reverse transition will pose no problem. If, on the other hand, you start by the passage, you may have trouble slowing the pace down to the piaffe without encountering such irregularities as magpie jumps, though the return to the passage will now be easier.

Introduction to either air is out of bounds until collection has ceased to be problematic, presupposing good impulsion and general relaxation of a horse suppled laterally by work on two tracks and on the circle, longitudinally by rein backs and speed variations within the same pace, particularly at the trot. The speed of the trot can thus be decreased to the limit: to where the horse has virtually ceased to advance. Needless to say that any exertion of force by legs and/or hands is banned. The horse must respond to light leg actions, combined with a softening of the fingers, by lengthening stride without precipitation, and by slowing down in response to a hand as light, without loss of rhythm, preserving good impulsion and balance at all times. Look upon the horse's joints as being veritable "springs" the flexibility of which must be coupled with impulsion, closely and in equal proportions. Obviously, if impulsion exceeds flexibility, the movement will die at the point where the slowdown exceeds the degree of flexibility, as it will also vanish when dwindling impulsion can no longer animate the "springs." But once your long and patient work has led to maximum and flawless slowdowns at the trot, broaching passage and piaffe should pose no major problems.

Passage

The essential difference between trot and passage is the extended duration of the time of suspension. This is achieved by the delay of the diagonal's rise from the ground, accomplished by shifting onto it some of the weight of the opposite shoulder. To wit, after a good lengthening you slow the trot to the maximum, and when the left diagonal is on the ground, your right rein bears on the neck from right to left. This hand action causes the burdening of the left shoulder and an equal lightening of the right, thus delaying the rise of the left diagonal, to be repeated by the left hand when the right diagonal is on the ground, ever respecting the rhythm of the pace.

Initially, place your horse on the left rein, on a circle (about 8 meters in diameter) and work each diagonal separately, in a light half shoulder-in position (on three tracks). With his left diagonal on the ground, the right neck rein will combine with the action of your left leg at or slightly forward of its normal place, the right rather a little in back to prevent the haunches from shifting to the right. These aids, which cease when the right diagonal is posed, are repeated when the left once more reaches the ground. No sooner has your horse given you a slightly loftier beat of the right diagonal with a more pronounced time of suspension than you must yield and cherish him, then ask for one or two more beats of the same; always on the same rein and—to guard against unsymmetrical beats— never more than one or two without a rest. Reverse aids repeat this exercise on the other rein.

Should you have trouble obtaining a suspension more pronounced than at the trot, you may engage the horse in a counter-change of hand at a very slow trot, though under good impulsion. Little by little you reduce the right and leftward steps to the point where one sort immediately follows upon the other, until they grow so tentative that the horse, driven to the right by your left leg, is received by the right which sends it back to the left, and so forth. Needless to say that in this case the horse must be maintained without *placer* and straight from head to dock. It is a risky

Fig. 69. The Passage. Passage in its loftiest form, denoting superior impulsion. *Courtesy Col. Jean de Saint-Andre.*

enterprise, liable to teach the horse to "swing his haunches," a very grave fault. Therefore drop this procedure at the very first sign of obedience, and do without it if you possibly can.

The first strides at the passage obtained, very progressively increase their number on both straight and curved lines. In theory, the slowing of the passage, the gradual diminution of the scope of its strides, will lead to the piaffe; in practice it is easier for parallel work to teach the horse to mobilize his legs on the spot, thus leading by and by into the trot on the spot (Fig. 69).

Piaffe

Your work begins on foot and continues under saddle, the point at which one seeks to link both airs. Again, the work on foot is preceded by flexions such as described in chapter VI.

The Work on Foot

First Exercise: Place yourself beside the horse's left shoulder, facing forward, your right hand holding the right rein slung over the base of the neck, the left holding the left rein at about 12 inches from the horse's mouth. A finger pressure on the reins at the halt prompts him to relax the jaw and flex at the poll before a click of the tongue asks for the walk under continued flexion. Acting more or less upward as needed, your left hand carefully maintains the proper head carriage, the poll remaining the highest point of the neck. Demand the halt from the walk, walk on again, halt again and rein back, the halt reduced to a minimum, and from the rein back once more walk on. When this exercise is performed with ease, in continued lightness, jaw relaxed, you may repeat it at the trot, though at absolute minimum speed and with primary attention to the improvement of the rein back to trot and trot to rein back transitions.

Second Exercise: Standing left of the horse at the halt, now facing backward, take the reins in the left hand, about a couple of inches behind the mouth. Your right hand touches a hindleg with a longish whip at or a bit above the fetlock; some horses respond better to the whip if applied just above the hock. If this hind fails to lift, let him advance a bit and reward him at the slightest sign of obedience. If he lashes out, he must be punished, but actually it should not come to that. Here, more than on any other occasion, remember that in equitation it is always better to underdo than overdo, for in the first instance one can make repairs by "adding a dose," while in the second one cannot belatedly "reduce the dose" already administered and the mistake becomes irreparable. Remember furthermore that this exercise requires frequent rest periods and do not be excessively demanding, but content to see your horse respond to whip and click of the tongue by mobilizing his four legs in the slightest of advances. This exercise is continued until you obtain the mobilization of the diagonal bipeds, time when you may go ahead.

Third exercise: Facing backward as before, you test and increase if necessary your horse's trusting acquaintance with the touch of the whip on neck, back and now also his haunches. When you are satisfied, you endeavor to obtain the mobilization of his legs as before, though now by touching the top of his croup. These touches, effected in cadence with the mobilization of the diagonals, are designed, if you will pardon the lyricism, "to relieve the croup of its earthly weight."

Initially, let the horse place his head at his convenience; too high, it might impair the action of the hindlegs; too low, the forelegs would no longer rise. So you want to counter your horse's head carriage as little as possible, exercising just the necessary control to regulate the elevation of the beats.

The Work Under Saddle

Following some pronounced lengthenings, demand a few strides at the passage, slowing them down very gradually by diagonal aids, as previously explained: right rein bearing on the neck from right to left, with simultaneous action by the left leg when the left diagonal is on the ground.

After a moment's rest, a few steps of rein back and your legs prompt the forward movement while your hands oppose this movement, *much as would a filter.* If your horse performs a few sketchy beats of piaffe almost on the spot, glide into a brief passage, then yield and pat. Repetition will eventually lead to a few actual beats of piaffe followed by a few strides at the passage.

This achieved, proceeding in reverse, one slows the passage until it results in two or three beats on the spot, then moves forward.

Beyond just precision of hand and leg actions, which must be absolutely correct in form, intensity and synchronization with each other and with the movements of the horse, proper balance is imperative. Although not produced by the balance, without it the movement cannot materialize *correctly.*

Balance plays an essential, more important part in the piaffe than in most other movements. If, for example, on a horse trained to the passage, the rider's legs are able to create sufficient impulsion and his hands know how to turn this impulsion to effective use, the horse will passage - even if the balance were to leave something to be desired. Though, no doubt the quality would be wanting, the performance would take place. The same cannot be said for the piaffe, which is inoperable unless performed in the appropriate balance.

Your horse's balance but also yours, a gram more or less of your weight here rather than there, a flick of fingers, a flutter of calves at "the moment of truth"—if one is missing nothing remains. Technically, this makes the piaffe. Yet there is one more thing, shared by this movement with all others, whether simple or complex: the spirit of the art finding expression in a display of cheerful elegance by you and *lampros hippos*, your brilliant horse "acting as he would on his own when happy and taking pleasure in what he is about."* (Fig. 70).

---

*Xenophon

Fig. 70. The Piaffe. Although the joints of the hindlegs are well flexed, the lowering of the croup appears to be somewhat insufficient, an impression caused by the length of a slightly hollowed back. Yet note the horse's state of relaxation and the perfect diagonalization of his legs.

Fig. 71. Wrought-iron stirrup, 16th century

EPILOGUE

A Question of Accent

Some claim that an abyss separates the French and German Schools, others proclaim the exact opposite, so where lies the truth? As usual, between the two, although this overly concise reply, not to be ambiguous, requires a look at the equestrian past.

Apace with the civilization of which it is a part, any art, as any activity, goes slowly but inexorably through considerable change, even if the ground rules remain essentially the same. This without taking into account personal or ethnic differences of interpretation or expression, often only a matter of nuances, in their application. One is therefore hard put to state coldly that the two Schools are, or are not, at variance.

Theoretically and indeed logically they should not differ; for, as of the first half of the eighteenth century, the Germanic School adopted the principles laid down by La Guérinière in *Ecole de Cavalerie*. La Guérinière was not only French but the prototype of the Gallic tradition. Yet French and German interpretations of his principles in fact differ, if mostly in the mode of their application, because French and Germans differ in spirit as they do in language. Even within their national borders, Prussians and Bavarians on one side of the Rhine, Picards and Provençaux on the other, despite all they have in common, have their distinct emotional and intellectual makeups. So why wonder? Peoples as well as their horses are subject to this law of nature, owing to soil, climate and environment and, as concerns horses, to man-made selection purporting to breed the sort of animal best suited to his own needs and predilections. Thus it is only natural that different men on different horses will differ in style and form, as they differ in accent and syntax.

While, then, the principles of France became (first through the oral teaching at La Guérinière's and other academies across France, then through his treatise) those of the Germanic (that is, German and Austrian) School and remained so over the centuries, they underwent of course filtration through the Teutonic mind. One must moreover remember that until relatively recent times there existed no "international competition," and only the privileged few had occasions to glance across their own borders. French and Germanic riding styles inevitably drifted apart. Not until 1912 at Stockholm were equestrian events included in the Olympic Games, and only 1921 saw the founding of the F.E.I. Such frequent encounters, as shall be seen, were gradually to lead to a happy rapprochement.

Before any sort of approximate unity was in the offing, a veritable revolution in artistic equitation had taken place in France. Around the middle of the nineteenth century an equestrian genius, François Baucher, feeling compelled to "rethink" the entire structure of the art and to reexamine every single one of its traditional tenets, came up with an original method which opened up new horizons, and therewith novel means, to gifted horsemen. His disciples were many, inside and outside of France, among civilians as well as the cream of the cavalry.

On the negative side, since 1830 French classical horsemanship had definitively lost the guardian of its traditions, the fabled School of Versailles, and ironically, not the avowed innovator Baucher, but a member of the now defunct institution during its dying days, the Viscount d'Aure, would give its spirit the *coup de grâce*. D'Aure spearheaded a movement no less "revolutionary" than that led by Baucher, though going in a diametrically opposite direction. Sacrificing to the gods of fashion, he advocated simplification, an instruction qualified by contemporary wits as "riding for those in a hurry;" in a hurry, that is, to show themselves on horseback without any need to go through the tedium of the long and minute progression required by the School of Versailles.

Only the Cavalry School at Saumur now remained to take upon itself the guardianship of the country's equestrian tradition, although this role did not enter into its official attributions. Fortunately, a number of its écuyers, whose talent found within its walls the opportunity to evolve and manifest itself, preserved and transmitted to the world the equestrian heritage of France. But these were individuals, while an entire institution, the *Spanische Hofreitschule* of Vienna, faithful to the letter (if not quite the spirit) of the teachings of La Guérinière, exerted great influence on the Prussian riders who now went there to study, while the British and American military had access to the School of Saumur, which civilians at the time had not.

With the return of peace after the First World War, the differences between both Schools did not vanish completely but grew more faint, largely thanks to such prominent personalities as Generals Decarpentry and von Holzing of France and Germany, respectively, and the German technician, Dr. Rau. Their profound knowledge, artistic sensibility and scrupulous professional honesty provided savant equitation with renewed impulsion and helped it to reach its highest degree of perfection. The rules of dressage tests they developed were strictly observed, because at international competitions—far fewer in number than nowadays—these same men were constantly found among the members of the juries. One thus was assured of proper application faithful to the very spirit in which these rules had been established, beyond merely perfunctory abidance. And in this spirit, in Decarpentry's own words, "equitation blossomed into poetry."

Where the border had lain up to an earlier part of the twentieth century may best be pinpointed by two quotations, one from each side of it.

"The German School," wrote Decarpentry, "proclaimed its unswerving fidelity to the principles of La Guérinière whose *oeuvre* remained their 'equestrian bible,' while Baucher found himself qualified as 'the gravedigger of French equitation.'*

"In reality, if the Germanic School upheld the method—or rather the progression—of an eighteenth century master who was not of their blood, the application made of his procedures suffered alterations, less pronounced on the banks of the Danube than on those of the Spree, due to their own inherent ethnic differences.

"While stopping short of roughness, its riders tended to persist in their direct opposition to the forces of resistance rather than have recourse to their skillful dissociation. Where submissiveness was concerned, they demanded the horse's unconditional surrender rather than seeking his generous participation in perfecting the common task. Their mounts' strict exactitude of execution was prized over joy apparent in gesture and attitude."

Gen. von Holzing, Decarpentry's opposite number in Germany, wrote in April 1932: "In Paris we have had occasion to see the Olympic test performed by eight French riders...One of my predominant impressions was the following: the contact between the French rider's hand and the mouth of his mount is very fine and soft. The horses are very calm, they look very content with their lot and their riders. This results in a natural grace in their motion which persists even in the most complicated movements...Almost all eight horses had those greatly coveted qualities of absolute lightness and finest contact...We noticed three or four which, in position in light, steady and soft contact, were what by German principles would be called, on the bit. This fact would have earned them, at the *Grand Palais* or elsewhere, the highest marks from any German judge."

Note in passing that those were the times when an expert was still free to speak of "grace," a word unknown, at any rate unused, in today's equestrian world where the two late gentlemen quoted above would indeed look in vain for a performance to which it might apply.

To sum up, around 1937, a time when equestrian concepts on either side of the border were closest, the essential difference lay in the fineness

---

*Note that his accusers did not hesitate to adopt Baucher's invention, the flying change of leg at every stride, described by Mr. Seeger in their time as nothing but an "ambled canter." May he rest in peace.

of aids which in France just barely grazed a horse so highly bred and trained that it understood and keenly responded to its rider's intent. Again,
contemporary testimony best illustrates this.

At the Berlin Horse Show of 1936, Col. Lesage, then Chief Instructor of
the Cadre Noir, was invited by the Show's President to ride Lt. Pollay's
Olympic mount, Kronos. He did so at the spur of the moment and with
his accustomed discreet aids, but gaining a first impression of a heavy,
unresponsive animal. Incredulous, for this was an exquisitely trained
dressage horse who had just won the Olympic Gold Medal, he decided to
use, for just an instant, a more peremptory hand and more vigorous aids,
feeling his mount, in his own words, "grow as light as a bird" and continue so henceforth. "He's earned his medal," he was to comment. As he
then watched Kronos' trainer, Otto Loerke, with more manifest aids and
some use of his considerable weight, take him through a no less impeccable performance of all the movements of the Olympic test, Lesage took
note of the obvious: "He is riding him the German way. I rode him à la
française."

Fig. 72. Major Lesage on *Taine*. Both horse and rider are in the relaxed, classical
posture which signals a state of ease and lightness under very slight contact sufficient to maintain a happy mouth.

Fig. 73. Major Gerhard on *Absinth*. The impression, perhaps to a point misleading, is of a stiff rider, an attitude reflected in the horse. As in the preceding photograph, the tail is not twisted but blows in the wind.

Fig. 74. First Lt. Pollay on *Kronos*. The same ease and lightness which we saw in the picture of the Frenchman. As did *Taine*, this horse is holding up his forehand, contact of just "the weight of the rein" suffices, with no need for more lest the horse lean on it. *All three Courtesy of the French Olympic Committee.*

PART 2:

A Guide to Basic Dressage

XVII.
"To Dress a Horse"

"A New Method and Extraordinary Invention to Dress Horses and Work them According to Nature by the Subtlety of Art," by William Cavendish, Duke of Newcastle, London, 1667.

The Duke was not an early wag, preoccupied with "decency for animals," he simply used the equestrian term, "to dress," for the word, training, as did everyone else in his time. The verb has vanished from the English language but the noun, "dressage," has received a frightful buffeting. Dressage to the average modern rider is a competitive event. Yet dressage means nothing except training, the training of the horse, not the rider, who is supposed to know what he is doing before he ventures to teach his horse. The French word for breaking in is *débourrage* (characteristically originating in the ordinary, everyday sense of cleaning, scraping, smartening up). The French for training is *dressage*, describing not only the period following the breaking in, but also, as does training, the entire education.

The title of the Newcastle book is, in itself, a capsule lesson in the meaning of dressage, as it adds, "and work them according to nature by the subtlety of art." It could not be better expressed, defining the very essence of the craft of dressage and, ultimately, the art of *haute école*, as distinguished from circus riding. Both exclude all but natural movements, performed by the horse spontaneously at liberty. Dressage proposes to stylize them and *haute école* carries them to perfection.

Haute école, then, is the "higher education" of a horse, provided by "teachers of high academic standing." It should not be confused, as it too often is, with what we call dressage, and the French call, *basse école* (low, as opposed to high, school), the horse's "secondary education." It is with this secondary level that this book is concerned.

We will begin at the beginning, acquire the proper horse, then learn to train him, step by step. The "dressage test" is just exactly what it declares itself to be: a test of training. So let us think of training only, until we have done the work up to the point where we may submit it for the consideration of a judge. Then we will begin to think of what to do and not to do in the arena. Go along with me without skipping and I do not think you will regret it; for there is no such recipe for instant dressage as "take a few pupils, add an equal amount of horses, place all of it into a school, pour over it the counsel of a teacher and let steep for three or four days." On the other hand, dressage is, as I said, a craft and thus it can be taught and learned in simple terms by relatively simple means, provided the student has already a good seat, steadiness, independence of aids and a certain feeling, called equestrian tact. Besides this he must be willing to work. If it is true that one can lead a horse to water but cannot make him drink, it is true that one can teach a rider but cannot make him learn. Personal work is all the more essential in horsemanship, on any level, because riding is not a purely mental skill. It cannot be absorbed entirely just by reading, listening, or even watching.

I am myself an avid reader and writer of equestrian books and articles and so I have no axe to grind when I warn you off excessive armchair equitation. My point is that if you cannot feel what you do not understand, you cannot understand what you do not feel. Both capacities develop together. I shall try, from chapter to chapter, to make you understand what you begin to feel, if you will try to feel what I give you to understand.

Shopping for a Horse. With a good seat, steadiness, independence of aids and a measure of equestrian tact you can enter into dressage, aiming to ride a horse competently in the elementary tests. But for this purpose you do not want an entirely green horse, which would require the employment of an experienced trainer if he was not to be spoiled. On the other hand, you do not wish to perform, like a couple of windup toys, with a mount trained from A to Z by someone more knowledgeable than you; anyhow, it cannot really be done. Neither do you want a too highly trained horse; you would not speak or understand each other's language and the end would be the ruin of both of you. What you do want is a six- to seven-year-old having had as good and rational a basic training as you should have received.

This kind of training is easily recognizable when you try the horse under saddle. He should be quiet, not sluggish, go forward freely without need of whip or spur, turn as easily to the left as to the right, and at all three gaits accept the contact with the bit on normal rein tension. He must look where he is going, not coiling his neck as though searching for a four-leaved clover, nor raising it to study cloud formations. While keeping definite contact with the hand, he should not pull at it or expect it to carry his head for him, nor must he move his head about at halt or in action. A jaw opening and closing constantly, or a lolling tongue, eliminates him from the picture, because these difficulties are almost impossible to overcome.

So he is well-behaved and apparently well-intentioned; but will his spirit and conformation let him progress along the path you have chosen? If he is to become a dressage horse he must be reasonably calm. It is possible for a very skillful trainer to get some use out of a high-strung, skittish, timid sort of horse in time, but even he will never be safe from unpleasant surprises in the arena.

Though there are fine and even outstanding mares on the dressage scene in general it is well to remember that geldings tend to be more even-tempered. This much for character.

Physically, he should, as any riding horse, have good natural balance. For *manège* work we want to see the top of the croup slightly lower than the top of the withers. This is the ideal, although we may accept withers and croup of equal height if all else is equal. Never, however, buy a potential dressage horse who stands higher behind than in front.

An easy, quick way of judging conformation is to check that the distance between the back of the withers and the front of the croup is reasonably short and that the distance between the point of the shoulder and the last false rib is fairly long. Most important, however, is the difference between these two distances: the greater the difference the better the horse.

This standard of proportions almost guarantees several qualities which, when examined separately, require more judging experience than most of you will have at this stage. If the distances in themselves and their relationship to each other are good, we usually find a good withers, not only high but (this is essential) stretching well back; not too much length in back and loins; a long, sloping shoulder, endowing the horse with good balance, and a deep chest.

Having examined those two distances and their relationship, we can look at the neck, which should be rather long, well muscled, but not thick, and carry a head of proportionate size. Too heavy a head makes the horse weigh on the hand and robs him of elegance while thick jowls prevent proper head carriage. Excellent points, however, are a neck well hung on (in other words, well oriented in emerging from the body) and a head well set onto this neck. An ewe-neck disqualifies outright; no amount of work will set it right. If you are curious to know in what position the fully trained horse under the saddle will eventually carry his neck at walk, trot and canter, you only need to note where he carries it naturally when trotting at liberty.

While you have him at the trot, look at his tail. Normal carriage indicates energy and good muscle tone at the top line. If it is too high there is stiffness on the top line and possibly some incorrect muscular development. If he clamps his tail between his buttocks it is a certain indication of stiffness somewhere and obviously it will affect his action.

Look at his way of going at the trot; profile, front and rear. If he crosses his legs, do not take him. If he dishes you will have trouble and he will never reach extended gaits. Ideally, his way of going should be true, but a little turning in of the toes may be overlooked.

Concerning the formation of the legs at the halt, it is important that the horse should stand square on all four feet. Avoid sickle hocks, or a horse whose forelegs slant to the rear at halt and come almost beneath the center. Finally take a good look at his feet—"no foot, no 'oss."

Then pay some general attention to elegance and size. In dressage tests, elementary or advanced, elegance is a factor and judges tend to be impressed by it. Size does not necessarily make for elegance but it enhances whatever there is of it. The gaits of a very small horse tend to convey a more cramped appearance, especially when following a taller entry whose speed-ups and slow-downs, though not actually better, will look more generous. Seek as much elegance, then, as you can afford, without sacrificing the more basic qualities.

Now have him vetted; the expense may save you far more costly surprises. Only the veterinary surgeon can assure you that your prospective purchase, who travels as much on his heart and lungs as on his legs, is organically sound. And only he can confirm that he has good eyesight. This is an important point, for often the horse scared of a tree is the one who does not recognize it for what it is.

To sum up, we want a horse sound in mind and body, of harmonious proportions, somewhat elegant bearing and with considerable mettle under a rather substantial frame.

First Acquaintance. The cliché of the road to success being long and hard is nowhere truer than here, when the partnership is first opened between horse and rider. So, if you are very young, I would say, "Arm yourself with patience;" if you are a little older, "Never let patience slip." Training for showing—whether in dressage, jumping, or eventing—is but the process of forming, improving and maintaining a loyal, unwavering partnership for better or for worse.

At the formation stage do not be overanxious for progress. Use the first week or so to become mutually acquainted. Here you have a great advantage over the horse. You may feel a bit strange on his back but this is a purely mechanical problem and is easily overcome in a few days. For him, on the other hand, everything is new and strange. As a result of his move his appetite and digestion may be a little affected and he may appear to be restless or jittery in his box, which won't help him to get a good night's sleep. He is tense and nervous when you want to ride him, not in anticipation of having you on his back, but following a bad day and night in the box. It may be that he will brood over his former stables, his past companions or his old groom, and when you ride him you may feel let down because he moved so much better when you tried him at his home stables. But give him time and let your behavior, your gestures, your voice, your care of him, all encourage him to put his trust in you. So long as he is not visibly glad to see . you in the morning and does not leave his box with a certain joyfulness, do not ask him for anything. Just go hacking, day after day, long outings at slow gaits, allowing the utmost freedom of the neck, though never losing contact with the mouth.

The main purpose of these hacks is to deepen the relationship between the two of you and they are not a waste of time. It will take two or three weeks, sometimes longer, before you can truly begin to work; but the hacks will always go on. By and by they will take on the name of *work*, as opposed to *lessons*, which take place in the school or arena. There must be no confusion about this. *Work* is a physical health exercise and keeps keenness intact or if necessary improves it. It is protracted but never overtaxing. *Lessons*, on the other hand, teach and improve the movements. They are short, never monotonous and are always broken by brief rest periods.

Though quite distinct, work and lessons are obviously related and therefore are interdependent. So each must be given with due regard for what happens in the other. If, for example, your horse lacks energy or keenness, you will quite naturally play down the lessons for a while and emphasize the outdoor work, it being normal for a rather unambitious horse to be less eager to deliver up his impulsive forces between four walls. Conversely, if he is the sort who is distracted at the drop of a pin, inattentive to orders, or a little too dashing for your taste and comfort, you should put rather more stress on the indoor lessons. It is up to you to know him sufficiently to apply the right means for his education.

Proof of success is a horse equally keen, disciplined and attentive both indoors and outdoors.

XVIII.
RIDING IN TUNE

We have discussed what we expect of our horse, and it is now time to consider what he expects of us in school and arena. First of all, leadership, knowing what we want and knowing how to convey our will to him. It is not enough to know the music, we must play it for him in key and without hitting the wrong notes because we have become wrongly positioned in relation to our "keyboard," or because a jolt unhinges us or keeps us from measuring our impact.

This brings us to the *position* in the saddle. A good one adds to the grace of the whole picture but its function is far more than that. A good position gives precision, effectiveness and discretion to the aids. Dressage tests demand proof that horse and rider have reached a level of training where they can execute a well-defined sequence of certain movements in close succession, not only without effort, but with ease. To do so, we must be able to change our aids swiftly without impairing the horse's balance and without the motions in themselves becoming obvious.

The horse's center of gravity runs along a vertical line going through the withers, so that the closer you sit to it (i.e. to the pommel of your saddle), the less you will feel that movement of the gaits and the easier it is to be with your horse. Do not stiffen up or let yourself go but hold yourself up straight, shoulders squared, head erect and well out of your shoulders. Let your arms drop naturally along your body, elbows bent, wrists held up in prolongation of the forearms, fingers closed over the reins, thumbs uppermost, fingernails face to face. Thighs, legs, toes drop normally by their own weight. The tread of the stirrup should be in a line with your ankle when your feet are out of the irons and allowed to go limp. When the foot is placed in the iron the toe must point upwards. You are sitting properly when an imaginary line passes from ears over shoulders, over hips, to heels.

This long explanation is as basically necessary to equitation as the multiplication table is for mathematics, and before you can go any farther it must have become the only natural and comfortable way of sitting for you. Now let us look at the details.

If you carry your *head* properly (high), looking in the direction you are taking, your overall position can hardly be all bad and changes of direction, also, are made easier. If you lower your head looking at your hands, everything goes wrong: the shoulders slump, the back hunches, the hands recede to your stomach, your seat moves towards the cantle, your legs advance and the changes of direction lose precision, the horse seeming to "drift" rather than to move with precision.

As to the *seat* itself, you do not sit in the saddle as you would on a chair. Your buttocks must be pushed forward under you; if you sit as though on a chair you are poised on the crutch. Sitting properly, you have good adherence and can use your seat as a third aid to complement the hands and legs.

The *loins* are for the rider what the shock absorber is for a car. If you stiffen them they cannot play their part and you will bounce at trot and canter. The small of the back must play freely in all directions if you want your seat to remain in place and go with your horse, and feel what is going on underneath you. If we speak of the "aid" of the seat, rather than that of loins or back, it is because it is your seat which acts in contact with the horse, not your back, the action of which is but a consequence of that made by the seat. It is your seat which encourages, promotes, accompanies or opposes the movements of the horse. In other words, the role of the loins is subordinate to that of the seat, not vice versa.

As to the *legs*, one does not stick on by pressing knees in to the saddle, but through suppleness. The legs must be in close contact with the horse but they must not cling to him. The more points of contact you have with your horse the closer you are to him, and the closer you are the more contact you will have. So you want to keep your whole leg, particularly the lower part, in contact with the flank but without squeezing. If you press with your knee the lower part of the leg cannot help but shoot outward and lose steadiness. If your legs do not keep this permanent gentle contact they will, when used as aids, necessarily act by fits and starts, and any subtle nuance in their use becomes impossible. Your horse will not be in the channel of the aids but will be able to escape your control; perhaps only by just a little, but a little is too much.

The *toes* are raised, mark my words, the heels are not lowered. To all appearances, but it is only to appearances, the result is the same. When the toes are dropped naturally so that the stirrup tread is at ankle height and you slip your foot into the stirrup, it is your toes which are raised, not your heel that is lowered. Your heel remains where it was, that is, somewhat below the stirrup tread. "Heels down" is a consequence, not an end in itself. If, hearing this command, you push them down, you stiffen the thigh and leg muscles and contract the knee and ankle joints which makes it hard for you to use your legs efficiently. Raising your toes tightens a single muscle in front of the leg, between knee and ankle, which does not hamper their freedom of movement.

XIX.
UNDERSTANDING THE AIDS

We have analyzed why only the classical position can provide a stable base for effective and precise use of the aids—aids which are discreet while being unmistakable in their clarity.

Hands and legs are our chief aids, the combination being completed by that of the seat.

Speaking of legs, we mean calves, heels and, if need be, spurs, the ultimate spokesmen for the legs. The spurs have their place on the training ground where they are used to make the horse sensitive to, and respectful of, our legs, making him respond by producing the desired movement or by giving greater impulsion. Their use is delicate at all times, and on the day we enter the arena we had better keep them strictly decorative. The whip is officially banned from the dressage arena, but it is used during early training and then again during advanced work, in hand. In our kind of work we may say, as they do at Saumur, that "legs are for the horseman, whips for the handicapped."

Both hands and legs operate by *acting, resisting* or *yielding*. The impulsion generated by the legs is received by the hands which control, regulate and filter it, just as though the horse were a steam boiler, the legs being the fuel and the hands the safety valve.

The hands—controlling this impulsion by regulating speed and giving direction—act by varying finger pressures and there is no need for them to remain other than still. Since the reins pass underneath the fifth finger and come out between thumb and index, their tension is changed and controlled by the opening or closing of the last three fingers. Using these fingers separately or in combination is like "playing" an instrument which the thumb and index finger have "tuned" when they closed at a chosen point on the reins. There are infinite nuances in changing rein tension. Let the little finger yield on its own for example, then try two fingers and then yield with all of them. Learning to play these nuances is learning to ride, learning to play them subtly is becoming a proficient rider. Wherever you may stand between these points there is no need to move your hands when riding a reasonably trained horse.

The hands *act* when they slow down the pace, or check it to a lower one, as from canter to trot. They act, also, to bring the horse to halt, to ask a rein back or to change direction. The hands *resist* by fixing themselves at a given spot *like a wall*, a fact which makes them very potent, yet less irritating to the horse than would be a live and moving force. They *yield* when the fingers slacken to decrease rein tension and they follow the movements of neck and head. But they can do nothing unless they do it on an "adjusted" rein, that is, one that is taut and even and through which the contact with the mouth is being channeled.

We might say that the legs, in the same way, must be "adjusted." In other words, they must be in permanent contact with the flanks, which is a contact as infinitely variable as that of the hands with the mouth, and is greatly dependent on the sensibility of the horse and the tact of the rider.

The legs, like the hands, can as I said before, act, resist or yield. They act simultaneously and together, to increase impulsion or speed or to pass to a stronger gait and they act in the same way to obtain the engagement of the hind legs. The single leg acts to shift the haunches one way or another. The legs resist, and this also is like a wall, to oppose a movement of the horse's initiative, such as an unwanted shift of haunches. They yield by relaxing or by ceasing to act or to resist, but always they keep a light contact and are ready to intervene if necessary.

Here I would put an end to the nonsense we hear all too often about owning a horse "too sensitive for contact with the legs," one who goes wild at their mere approach. This same "sensitive child" is expected to accept on his back a weight which is not always as steady as it might be and which is far more keenly felt than the light contact of legs, and he must also put up with hands acting on his mouth, not always tenderly, by means of a piece of steel. Of course, he will accept the legs providing his rider can apply them steadily and in a controlled fashion.

Take a young horse, barely backed and not having felt the legs at all. Spread your legs from knees to heels so as to prevent even the faintest contact, then approach his flanks with both simultaneously, applying pressure very gradually with equal intensity once the legs are touching the flanks. If the pressure is coming on gradually, continuously, smoothly, nine out of ten horses won't move.

Hence the horse does accept unambiguous contact with the legs just so long as they do not shift about. Pressure, after all, does not automatically entail forward movement and the various forms of leg action have no natural significance to the horse, who has to be taught their meaning. So ride with your legs in contact, and if the horse will not accept this go back and teach him to accept the legs as he was taught to accept the bit and body weight before you undertake anything more.

The Aids: How? "Now bring back your right leg," or, "At this point, the rider should act with his left hand. . . . " Teachers frequently speak or write in this way about the *which, when* and *where* of the aids but their pupils do not always achieve the proper results because they have not learned *how* these aids should be applied. Yet it is only, in reality, a matter of mastering certain basic skills; believe me, it is nothing to do with magic.

Hand action, for example, depends largely on shoulders and arms, because the reins extend from the horse's mouth along your arms all the way up to your shoulders. The contractions of your shoulders, therefore, run down along the arms and reins, reverberating in the horse's mouth. You must, therefore, learn to relax the shoulders and to *keep* them relaxed, holding your elbows close to your body, your arms dropping naturally from shoulders to elbows, if the rein tension is not to change constantly. You will not notice these changes in tension but the horse will, and he will react accordingly.

Rigidity, or instability, in these parts of the body must be eliminated because they interfere with your hands' first duty which, whether they are acting, resisting or yielding, is to develop, improve and safeguard a soft mouth. The disappearance of this quality in the mouth instantly affects the horse's general behavior and his performance of movements and gaits. What is more, it shows. More often than not a hard mouth is due to a lack of softness in our hands—and if we want to be sure of never pulling, we must not retract them at any time. Rather, increases in rein tension must be made solely by finger pressures, reinforced, if necessary, by resisting shoulders. Whatever the resistance we make with our hands must be strictly commensurate with that put up by the horse and it must cease *instantly* the moment he yields. *"A main galante, bouche galante"*—gallant mouth to gallant hand!

Leg action, while as delicate and finely shaded as that of the hands, is much less natural to the horse, who must be trained to understand it. It should take the form of brief, recurrent taps, ranging from weak to strong—mere pulsations, in fact, of the calves at the bottom of the scale, spur attacks at the top, both resembling the staccato of the hammer of an electric bell, not the continuous action of the pneumatic drill.

The effectiveness of the leg in obtaining the forward movement, its main function, depends on the horse's sensibility and generosity, and on his training and your own. That is, you must have learned how to make proper use of your legs. The principal problem of the forward movement, however, is psychological. The horse must be made to understand from the beginning that at the quiet *prompting of the legs* he must move forward, an awareness which must eventually be sharpened to the point where he advances at the mere *permission of the hands*, the legs remaining, so to speak, in reserve.

At first we can go so far as to sacrifice the otherwise essential contact with the mouth, and, if reaction to the initial request of the legs is not forthcoming with due promptness, let progressively stronger action follow on the spot in the way of taps with the calves, the heels, and then, if need be, the spurs or even the whip. It is clearly pointless, and even dangerous, to set the horse on the bit *before* the forward movement has become truly automatic for the reason that hand and bit at one end combining with ineffective leg action at the other is only likely to cause restiveness in the animal.

The efficiency of the action of the single leg, shifting the haunches, is a matter of timing rather than degree. In a half-turn on the forehand, for example, you cannot expect your horse to move his near hind, for instance, at the prompting of your left leg if you apply it at the very moment when he is carrying his weight on that particular limb. If, on the other hand, your leg acts at the moment when the horse's off-hind is carrying his weight and his near-hind is therefore free, then the crossing of the legs will be made easy for him. The same is true, of course, when working on two tracks.

Nevertheless, you must also remember that the action of the leg to shift the haunches is different from its action when asking for forward movement. In the first instance the leg acts to the rear, in the second from rear to front. Both these movements should in time be minimal and eventually invisible though they must always be entirely obvious to the horse.

These are movements which must be learned, so do not hesitate to exaggerate them at first by spreading your legs and then, for the forward movement, taking them back a little in order to bring them forward again to their normal place under an increase of pressure which gives the movement a somewhat rounded character. The same thing, in reverse, is carried out when the leg asks for a shift of the haunches. But remember that the thighs and knees remain in place, they should never take part in the action of the lower leg.

Of the seat we may expect no more at this point than that it should be supple enough to remain with our horse in movement and balance, the flexibility of the small of the back keeping us from bumping in the saddle. In other words, for the time being, we look upon it as a passive aid.

What we can do, though, by looking where we are going, whether on straight lines or curves, is to weight, automatically, the saddle in the right place at the right moment, thus making sure that we do not disturb the horse's balance. This is done by slightly advancing the outside shoulder on a curve so that the body faces the direction in which we are traveling. The right shoulder, for example, would be advanced when circling to the left and vice versa.

This transference of weight, putting more emphasis on one buttock than the other, is only one or two forms of intervention by the seat. There is also the more accentuated movement made to push the horse on in his current gait, or a lesser body movement allowing the pace to remain unaltered. Further by these means we can oppose an unwanted initiative on the part of the horse.

We can, as an example, without changing the position of the upper body, make one buttock bear more weight than the other, a very keenly felt difference for the horse, since the weight added to one side is taken off the other.

Our normal movement when staying with the horse at the canter may be exaggerated in order to drive him on, or it may be diminished when the sole aim is to remain at the current gait. Then, so that we shall not counteract the movement of the rein back, we will allow our seat to follow the movement felt, very lightly; whereas at the halt, our seat is blocked to keep the hind legs engaged.

But before you can feel you must learn, and before you can learn you must feel, and for some time this will be your problem should you want to use the seat as an "active aid."

Independent but in Concert. In reviewing how our hands and legs can act, resist or yield we have been looking at the positive side of the question of aids, on the premise that the negative has been resolved. Alas, this is not always the case. As yet it is unlikely that we will have reached the stage where our hands and legs are under such perfect control that they can be used accurately and precisely without being upset by the horse's reactions. Our quest for this control is complicated by the fact that it is extremely difficult to move a particular hand or leg without it affecting the other limbs. If you try to make a few asymmetric movements with your arms you will realize how hard it is. When you have to think about your legs, too, it is even more difficult and, not surprisingly, the difficulty increases when you are on a horse and your legs are expected to make different and independent movements.

This is why we should not for the moment attempt to use extremely refined or complicated aids. We are incapable of doing so, even if we have the most complete theoretical knowledge, for the simple reason that our limbs cannot translate into physical action the theory absorbed by our brains. Our best plan, from now and all the way to the top, is to improve the functioning of our aids up to perfection on the current plane, and only after that has been achieved to move on to the one above. *The independence of the aids* is contingent on the seat, without which we cannot stay "with" our horse. Our seat must be sufficiently supple and pliable to allow us to remain relaxed enough to operate the aids smoothly. A good seat, however, is not sufficient, unless accompanied by steadiness which, conversely, is unthinkable without a good seat. Only if we are steady in the saddle will we avoid making unnecessary and, perhaps, harmful movements. But steadiness is not synonymous with immobility; we are steady in relation to our moving horse. Steadiness in equestrian terms is not a static quality.

Our aids must, like a football team, work "independently but in concert," so if one of the keys to equitation, as we already know, is the good balance of the horse, the other is *good coordination of the aids*. Gaspar de Saunier told his contemporaries that he overheard a French nobleman ask the great eighteenth-century master, Duplessis, to teach his son, "not to be an *écuyer*, just to coordinate his hands and legs with what he had in mind," then he quoted the master's reply, that this had been the object of his own search "for these past sixty years," and that he was still searching for it.

After just a few months' riding, every movement will require the participation of both legs and both hands. Each leg has a well-defined assignment of its own which is quite distinct from its partner, and the same is true of the hands, one of which is always either permitting or reinforcing the action of the other. At first we only try to keep legs and hands from making the worst mistakes, then we go through a transitional period where these bad reflexes are no longer so much of a problem but where applying the aids correctly demands some thought, which usually results in the aids being applied a little late. Eventually it is the good habits we have learned that predominate, but, of course, there is still, as always, room for improvement.

Until well into the second phase most riders tend to make too much use of their hands and too little of their legs, though the role of the hands is quite clearly subsidiary to the action of the legs. Nevertheless, since both are equally necessary, neither should predominate to the exclusion of the other but should operate in proper coordination.

Doubtless, the instructor's explanations will be helpful in teaching us to use our hands and legs in such a way and sequence as to obtain a specific movement. But this help can only be given preparatory to the actual movement, since once we are in motion the aids must move more swiftly than he can voice his advice. For there is just one right, precisely timed, instant to act, and the same aids applied either before or after that split-second of truth will, at best, be ineffective. At the worst they can run counter to the horse's action and become downright negative. Another thing the teacher cannot indicate, and this is the great problem, is the strength of intensity of the aids at any particular moment or for any particular movement. He cannot do so because it is not he but the ever-changing horse who dictates from one moment to the next the intensity of the aid we must apply. Finally, there is the feel of the horse. Only the rider can sense its impulsion, balance or lightness at any given moment, and only he can sense incipient resistance. If a resistance reaches the proportions of being noticeable, then, certainly, the instructor can help, but the slight, incipient resistance can only be detected by the rider.

Give and Take. There are several terms used to classify the aids. We use the words *natural* and *artificial* to distinguish between hands and legs and whip and spurs; we say *upper* and *lower*, meaning hands and legs, and we also talk about *active* and *passive* aids, those that either act, resist, yield or limit. Then there are the *lateral* and *diagonal* aids, when either hand and leg on the same side act, or when they do so on opposite sides. We will all be familiar with these terms, but really only two apply in practice: the active and passive and the lateral and diagonal aids.

The concept of active and passive aids is particularly interesting, because so few riders are aware of what it implies, and even the enlightened ones do not always apply their knowledge. The main implication is that one must know how to give, which few seem able to do, although everybody, somehow, knows how to take.

Every time a hand acts, the more so if both do, this action may be compared to that of a brake. Consequently, it provokes a slowing down. The decrease in pace may not be immediately evident nor a very pronounced one, but at least morally the horse senses an opposition to the former movement. If the hand action is wrong, he will fight it, more or less promptly, in one way or another. Either he will withdraw his impulsive forces or he will pull in order to escape. In any case, we shall be no longer in a position to control him correctly and a struggle will ensue. The horse will stiffen up and contract himself, and so most likely will we. It is a vicious circle. If he balks, and we are no longer raw beginners, we use our legs to drive him "onto the hand;" and many instructors, no longer raw beginners either, will let it go at shouting "Legs, legs!"—which is far from sensible. Beware of slogans used out of context—they are dangerous things.

If the horse balks because he fears a hand too hard for the sensitivity of his mouth we shall not overcome the difficulty by using our legs to push him even more energetically onto this ignorant hand. On the contrary, we shall only increase his exasperation. In short, we must know when and how to use our legs, and, furthermore, with what intensity they can be used in relation to our hand.

If our hands are "intelligent," and we know how to make them so acceptable to the horse that he trusts them, the legs have a minimal part to play. If they are not and tend to provoke a struggle each time they come into use then the legs must be extraordinarily strong to make the horse accept contact with the bit. Even if this can be done the effect is one of force-cum-resistance and will be rightly penalized in a dressage test.

Undoubtedly, the part played by the legs is important, since it is they which create the forward movement without which riding becomes impossible. In the case of beginners, who invariably ride more with their hands than their legs, the instructor's slogan "Legs, always the legs, and again the legs," is used in the correct context. In this instance the teacher is trying to inculcate the idea of forward movement into his pupils just as the trainer does with his horse.

There comes, however, a time when both horse and rider must understand more subtle implications; when the effect our legs have on the horse becomes more moral than physical. The trainer, when he works his horse in hand, or on the lunge line, is not pinching him between his legs and yet he obtains by a grazing with the whip or a clicking of the tongue the most perfectly free forward movement. Once he has inculcated into the horse the almost obsessive urge to advance at the faintest signal, it is up to the rider to use his knowledgeable, educated hands to permit and encourage this "fixed idea" to materialize.

Let us now take a look at some concrete cases and the bearing all this has on them. The hands yield when both legs act to create or augment impulsion (forward movement). The legs, on the contrary, yield when the hands act in order to slow down or halt the forward progression. One hand yields when the other acts to change direction or bend the horse; one leg yields when the other acts to shift the haunches.

These are truisms, for otherwise the aids would contradict each other. And yet, from the beginning we seem to run up against difficulties by failing *to yield before we act*. As an example, when we want our horse to walk out from the halt, our hands must yield *before* our legs act.

This kind of coordination of aids is simple; it does not require great experience, only a little forethought. But soon coordination must become more refined, more precise, and, above all, more complex. There is a great deal of food for thought in the fact that from the very moment the rider "intervenes" the management of the horse requires the use of his two hands and legs for any correct movement, and that his intervention begins the moment he sits down in the saddle.

Let me give you a little immediate food for thought by asking you to ride an imaginary left circle. Before doing so you will need some reserve impulsion, because by leaving the track and being ignorant of the direction he will be made to take, the horse will tend to slow down. Almost instantaneously your weight must enter into action by a slight advance of the right shoulder to keep you facing in this direction. Slightly forward of its normal place, your left leg, around which the horse will bend, attends to the impulsion. Slightly back, the right leg keeps the haunches from escaping to the right and makes them stay on the track you have chosen. The left hand flexes the neck just sufficiently to bend the whole horse in accordance with the circle's curvature and at the same time keeps the direction, while the right must yield at the start to let the left inflect the neck and must then resist to reinforce the action of the left hand and perhaps even help it keep direction by using a counter-rein. On top of everything else, both hands must unceasingly control the speed, regulate the impulsion, make sure the jaw remains relaxed and attend to the balance.

This is a random example of the problems involved in the coordination of the aids, and if the beginning-to-average rider tries to put it into effect in all its details he will fumble and fail and his horse along with him. Even if the average-to-proficient rider applies it correctly to the last aid, his horse, if not itself sufficiently trained, will still make a mess of it. Thus both horse and rider must have followed an adequate progression and have arrived at an adequate level of training before venturing anywhere near a dressage arena.

XX.

THE RIDER AS TRAINER AND THE FIRST COMMANDMENT

We have discussed the active and passive aids which are of particular interest in both the simplest form of riding and the highest reaches of dressage. In looking now at the *lateral* and *diagonal* aids, we shall be slipping a little way into the territory of training.

I told you at the start that I was providing you with a "trained horse," addressing you as a rider, not a trainer. But what is commonly called "the training period" is, in reality, a period during which the horse has learned just as much as his particular trainer intended to teach him, and the sum total of his attainment will depend on what level his trainer originally had in mind. The horse may, therefore, be trained to quite a high degree or, on the other hand and with a different trainer, still be almost green.

Here we suppose that your horse has been trained to the point where you can both take the final step towards the dressage arena; but if you think you can be just a user of a trained horse (that is, go for a ride on one without the slightest intention of furthering his training) you will be disappointed. No matter how "neutral" you may be you will not improve him, and you will probably finish up by ruining your mount. Since a horse is not a machine which can be regulated by a switch to a certain unchangeable level of efficiency we must touch on training matters even here.

Now, one of the schooling means are the lateral aids which should, whenever possible, be given preference in training. Even movements requiring the diagonal aids should, regardless of what this may do to the horse's position, first be worked on by lateral aids. The horse understands the lateral aids better and yields more naturally to them, while the constricting diagonal aids are liable to occasion struggle and delay.

Take the half-turn on the forehand, which requires the diagonal aids: on a right turn, action of the right leg (active aid) and the left counterrein (passive aid), to keep the shoulders from shifting left. Though it is only in this way that the movement can be performed properly, we should begin by using the lateral aids on the right: i.e. right leg and hand. The horse will slightly shift his shoulders to the left but will yield better to the action of the right leg by shifting his haunches to the left, and this is capital. Moreover, and above all, the forward movement won't be affected by his being caught between right leg and left hand.

Once he has understood the mechanics of the new movement, we may little by little go over to the diagonal aids.

The same is true for the departures at the canter. Before going on to the diagonal aids, we begin by using the outside lateral aids, once more disregarding the effect it has on the horse's position.

What matters in riding, even beyond training, is to make oneself understood by one's horse, and the simpler and clearer our requests the more easily will they be carried out by the horse.

The logical sequence from simple to complex is only part of what is called "methodical procedure." Another part is the setting aside while working on a new movement (however prepared the horse may be for it) all that is extraneous to it, so as to lay full stress on essentials and not to muddle up our aids.

"Never chase more than one hare at a time," be clear in your mind as to the primary purpose of each lesson, and of the means by which you plan to pursue it, and base the next lesson's program on its results. Ask for whatever is "new" at the end of the lesson so that the slightest obedience can be rewarded by sending your horse instantly back to the stables.

Rewards, and incidentally punishments, are of course particularly meaningful in training and though used less and more moderately in time, they never lose their importance. Reward should occur more frequently than punishment; for if we are patient, and do not ask for too much, we are naturally called upon to reward more often than to punish, while if we keep our horse too long under subjection we are bound to drive him to rebellion. This revolt is not always immediately apparent, at least not to the inexperienced who do not feel or the careless who do not want to feel. By the time it becomes overt, however, we may be unable to cope with it in a normal way and feel compelled to have recourse to punishment. Think how much simpler it would have been after ten minutes of attentive work or at the improved performance of a movement to reward by giving a few minutes' rest. Human nature tends to take for granted whatever is right and dwells only on what is wrong; and yet horsemanship, like lifemanship, gains immeasurably by a timely show of appreciation. Effort without recognition in both fields leads to apathy or revolt.

Punishment is much more delicate to administer, because, while the very motivation for reward tends to put us into a calm, good-natured frame of mind, punishment tends to be given in a state of incipient anger or impatience. And yet, more than anything else, it requires calm and perfect self-control. It must be given commensurate with the fault committed and a bare few seconds later equanimity must reign as before. The matter is further complicated by the fact that, while reward follows obedience, incipient or fully materialized, punishment often follows something that has not materialized. The horse may have failed to obey because he does not understand or because he is physically incapable. Punishment in such cases is out of place and very harmful because horses, like children, are especially sensitive to injustice and, having a great memory, resent the rider who administers punishment indiscriminately. Particular caution is necessary with young horses, where we must learn to distinguish between a buck, for instance, given out of malice or from sheer *joie de vivre*.

One thing is true for both reward and punishment; each must follow instantly the act which prompted them, and the wise trainer is the one who "requests often, is satisfied with little, rewards a great deal."

It is not by chance that I have concluded this first general discussion of the aids with a few pointers on method and psychology. If the effect of our aids is physically contingent on our seat and position, morally it is contingent on the horse's state of mind and our own—his preparedness and receptivity, our discipline and patience. Where all this is present calm exists, and calm is the point of departure, the only one, for action.

The First Commandment. The catechism of riding is short: "calm, forward and straight." These three commandments apply equally to horse and rider. Let us consider the first of this trinity.

Calm must always be present, not only when things are going well but when everything goes wrong. Most particularly, it must be present in the rider at the moment of punishment.

We know that calm is as communicable as nervousness, and that the horse, extremely impressionable animal that he is, detects in his rider the faintest wavering. Whenever we feel in danger of losing our calm we had better give the horse a rest for as long as it takes us to recover it. A certain firm believer in "the blessings of the timely cigarette," whom I knew, and himself a nonsmoker, used to carry a packet for exasperated pupils during difficult lessons. At any rate, if ever we lose our calm and cannot promptly regain it, we had better leave the school and go for a hack, or else alight and return the horse to the stables. It won't be wasted time; at worst no progress is made that day, but at least we have made no retrograde steps in our relationship with our horse.

If a calm outlook on the part of the horse is based upon his trust in his rider it follows that trust can only come about in an atmosphere of calm. This is so important that we should understand how a horse can acquire calm, develop it and even lose it.

To start with let us be quite sure that we do not, as many do, confuse a high-strung with a high-bred horse. The highly-strung is really a compulsive extrovert, the high-bred is a horse rich in physical, moral and mental qualities. Despite exceptions, it may be said that the Thoroughbred has a quicker understanding than a part-bred horse and that the quality of his tissues, bones and tendons tend to be superior. Also, he is "keen" and capable of producing great effort long after he has grown physically tired, because of the "courage" with which he is so amply endowed.

Even among these horses we will find extroverts, introverts, and normally constituted characters. The highly-strung horse reacts strongly to all or most sensory perceptions. He has, indeed, a moral and/or a physical vulnerability which can be expressed to a pathological degree. This state, which would be called "neurotic" in the human, is called "crazy" or "dangerous" when it occurs in the horse. We should no more trust or set our hopes in a crazy animal partner than we would in a neurotic human. But we have chosen a normal horse, as well balanced in body and mind as we think ourselves to be. But what about the stable yard atmosphere? Is our groom as calmly firm and firmly calm as we are? Or is he, without meaning any harm, frightening the daylights out of our perhaps young, certainly, at first, somewhat bewildered animal by loud guffaws and violent motions? Calm does not mean dull monotony, nor is it necessary to entertain our horse continually, but it is essential that he should be kept from growing bored. Too many horses when off work are stored away in a dark corner with nothing to see but a bare piece of wall, and here begins boredom which ends in mental, emotional and even physical sluggishness. Life in the stables should go along calmly but that does not exclude the horse from taking an interest in life. Playing a radio, if it is not up too loud, is a simple antidote to boredom and is appreciated by horses.

During work, however, all distractions are to be avoided, the horse's undivided attention must then be focused on his rider, or else the better part of what we are so painstakingly trying to instill will be lost on him. The ideal place for schooling is a covered school, where the horse can be immune to distractions and where we can work whatever the weather outside.

By taking sensible precautions to ensure that our horse is neither bored nor frightened in his stable and by never exceeding his capacity for concentration by working for too long at a time without rests all should go well, and calm will be preserved in both horse and rider.

XXI.
THE HORSE TURNS BY BOTH ENDS

At this point we should be sure of our aims and of our horse (and he sure of us). Also, we should by now be sure of our position and aids and of at least the first commandment of the riding catechism, absolute calm. This is not the first commandment because it is the most important of the three, but because until calm is complete we cannot begin any constructive work on the other two, or in fact, on anything else.

Assuming that we have reached this point we can now begin studying the different movements, starting with the one which is an integral part of nearly all of them, the change of direction.

One tends to forget that the horse may turn in three different ways. He does so by his body pivoting around the hind legs or around the forelegs or by both ends at once, all four legs shifting as he turns around a vertical axis located at the girth.

At liberty he does the latter because it is easiest for him. The first (half-turn-on-the haunches type) he will do on rare occasions, usually when he is frightened and wants to change direction abruptly and almost on the spot. The second (turning solely around the forehand) he can safely be said never to do of his own volition.

And yet this half-turn on the forehand is, if we want to make his haunches light, our first method of teaching him to yield to the single leg.

Why is this lightness of the haunches so important? Because the great and principal set of the *resistances* is in the haunches, where the "engine" is. Even when we find a lack of lightness at the front end it often has its origins in the haunches and so it is to them that we must return, making them shift laterally, swinging them from leg to leg, and then, quite often, the resistance in the forehand will vanish by itself.

Moreover, *changes of direction*, which positioning of the neck can only indicate, are actually imposed by the positioning of the haunches. To turn left, for example, your left rein bends your horse's neck left and makes him look to the left as well. But suppose he throws his haunches also to the left? He will be going to the right because whenever front and back end are in conflict the back end wins.

Why this happens is not hard to understand. Because head and neck can move independently of the rest of the body they are not sufficiently related to it to determine the direction of the shoulders. This movement is dictated by the haunches which are connected to the trunk. So let it be well understood that changes of direction are *prepared by positioning the haunches and then carried out with the head in the lead.* Count d'Aure used to say that one must pre-position the haunches as a sailor would his rudder in determining a change of course. This principle, far from applying only to young riders and/or horses, remains valid all the way to the Grand Prix Dressage Test.

In changes of direction initiated by the forehand, lightness, the great fetish of dressage, is lost, because the haunches keep driving in the original direction while the shoulders are taking another course. The haunches then form a sort of buttress, obstructing change and, no matter how light the horse had seemed in walking straight ahead, a more or less pronounced resistance appears as he starts into the change. The "harmony of the forces" is lost if we do not *pre-position the seat of impulsion for the change of direction and have the head and neck position instantly adjusted to it.*

How this lateral mobility of the haunches should be obtained will become clear in the half-turn on the forehand, which we shall discuss in detail. It is only when we are able to shift the haunches easily that we will be able to hold them in place for the half-turn on the haunches, correct circles, voltes, serpentines and other movements requiring the horse to move on curves.

The Half-turn on the Forehand. A half-turn on the forehand is carried out on the spot, one foreleg serving as a pivot (the off-fore when the haunches are driven to the left, the near-fore when driven to the right). All four limbs must be mobile, including the pivot leg, which, though it moves neither forward nor sideways, must lift and touch down on the spot whenever its turn in the four-time beat of the walk comes up.

To make sure of getting in the whole progression we shall assume that the horse is not yet accustomed to the single leg, the instrument we use (acting by itself behind its normal place) to shift the haunches or to oppose any unwanted movement on their part.

Our first aim is to teach him to cross his hind legs so that *the crossing limb passes in front of the crossed limb.* To do this the horse *must* be allowed to advance.

Let us deal with a concrete example. We want to obtain a left half-turn on the forehand, where the haunches are driven from right to left around the off-shoulder. Now if you will stop to reread and analyze this sentence the directions to follow will be clear. Whenever you want to apply them to the right half-turn, you just reverse the words *right* and *left*.

So now to work on the *left half-turn* which we shall do, first, on foot, to make it easier for both the horse and ourselves. We stand by his head on the off-side facing the croup, then take a pace or two backwards inviting him to advance with us by clicks of the tongue and sharp but not rough touches on the off-flank with a rather long whip held in the left hand. Both reins are held about four inches from the mouth in the right hand.

As soon as easy compliance is obtained in moving straight ahead—that is, when a couple of clicks without benefit of whip have repeatedly prompted the horse to walk out from the halt—we ask, again with the help of the whip, for a slight left shift of the haunches. He will better understand us if we draw his head a little to the right (towards us) and slow down the walk by a faint opposition of our right hand but *without ever letting him stop.*

No sooner has he given us a couple of forward steps, crossing his hind legs, than we let him rest a while and tell him by a pat that, though his movement was but a hint of things to come, he is headed in the right direction.

We finish up by reversing the aids, doing the same exercise in the opposite direction with the haunches now shifting from left to right, and at that point we bring the day's lesson to an end. Remember that all new things should come at the conclusion of the lesson so that an instant return to the stables can follow a satisfactory performance. We do this not only because the horse deserves a reward but because in this way the horse retains in his mind a sharp impression of the new movement.

The next step is to repeat the lesson in the saddle, combining the action of our right leg (quite far back to begin with) with that of the whip, applying both just where the latter was used during the work on foot. As before, we always work *going forward*, always slowing down from an active walk before prompting the lateral shift of the haunches. Eventually the horse will yield to the sole action of the right leg.

I hardly need to mention that at each of these stages the work is done on both sides, with more emphasis being placed on the side to which the horse has more difficulty in making the movement. Thus the horse will be made equally light to either hand. Once this point is reached we can think about improving the movement and begin the half-turn on the forehand, which is also called "half-pirouette in reverse."

For this purpose we use *reversed half-voltes*, the same basic figure as the half-volte, but, as the name implies, ridden in reverse. Instead of leaving the track by the half-circle and regaining it by the oblique track to the wall, as in the half-volte, we leave the track on the oblique line and regain it by riding the half-circle. (**Fig. 1**)

Keeping the example of the left half-turn on the forehand in mind, we start on the left rein and first ride an ordinary reversed half-volte in which the hind legs strictly follow the forelegs and the half-circle leading back to the track has an 18 ft. diameter. Then we start again but this

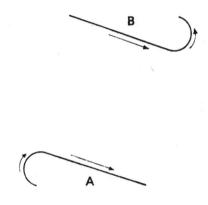

Fig. 1. (A) Half-volte and (B) Reversed half-volte.

time, at the end of the oblique and before starting into the half-circle which will bring us back to the track, we slow down the walk and simultaneously let our right leg act backwards in an effort to obtain a shift of the haunches to the left. By doing so we are driving the hind legs outside the track made by the forelegs.

We support the backward motion of our right leg by an equal advance of the left and we do not look at the leg which shifts the haunches. If we were to look to the right we would automatically be lightening the near-side of the horse and burdening the off-side. What we should be doing is precisely the opposite; our weight should be placed, of course, on the side to which the haunches are shifting.

By tightening the reversed half-volte little by little and making the half-circle gradually smaller, we reach the stage where we are executing a half-turn on the forehand at the walk.

Because the horse has never been allowed to stop, always being made to move forward, he has had to cross his hind legs properly by passing the crossing limb in front of the other and, as an added bonus, his forelegs, particularly the pivot leg, have remained mobile within a clearly marked gait of four-time, however slow the pace.

Only after he has become light in front, and thus well balanced, may we expect to obtain a good half-turn on the forehand at the halt. Even when this is achieved, however, the halt should never be extended if the pivot leg is to maintain its mobility.

The diagonal aids for the left half-turn on the forehand (around the off-shoulder) are as follows: slow down the walk; right leg back to demand shift of the haunches to the left (active aid); left counter-rein to keep the shoulders in place and avoid their shifting to the left; weight on the left buttock without impairing the straightness of the upper body; left leg at the girth to maintain impulsion. Finally, go again into the walk as soon as the half-turn has been fully executed.

Obviously, in acquainting our horse with the use of these aids we once more follow a progression. At first we only act with the leg which shifts the haunches (the right in our example); then we use a direct rein of opposition on the same side as the acting leg in order to block some of the shoulders' forward movement. This direct rein of opposition, also, contributes to the action of the leg, since it drives the haunches to the left.

Only when the shifting of the quarters from either leg has become satisfactory can we begin to use the diagonal (the classical) aids for the half-turn on the forehand.

XXII.
THE QUESTION OF BALANCE

One of the principal goals of training is the ability to change the horse's equilibrium as circumstances or movements dictate. Since even a competent trainer can only improve natural balance to a certain point, knowing how to recognize it in a horse which you contemplate purchasing is clearly important.

Balance depends on conformation and most particularly on the slope of the shoulder, and orientation of the neck, the formation of the legs and the proportions which make up the harmonious whole. For want of a better definition, we speak of the horse's "center of gravity;" but in reality there is no such fixed point in equitation. An animate body keeps this "center" in constant motion if only by breathing. There can be no exact method of determining where it is, nor is it possible to fix it in one place. The rider's attention, should, therefore, be focused on the consequence of these shifts in the center of gravity; the balance, in fact, which we shall learn to feel as we become more proficient.

The horse's weight, like that of a structure supported on pillars, is distributed over his four legs but, and this complicates matters, it is not evenly distributed because the pillars are not at the four corners, since the neck and head are in front of the forelegs. The weight of these two items and their shape and orientation must therefore influence the overall weight distribution. Experiments have shown that with a horse weighing 768 lb, holding his head and neck normally, the forelegs carry 420 lb and the hind legs 348 lb; that is, the forelegs carry 72 lb more than the hind legs. The same horse with head and neck lowered, increases the weight carried on his forelegs to 436 lb, his hind legs carrying, as a result, only 332 lb and the difference increasing from 72 to 104 lb.

When head and neck are raised, the weight on the front diminishes to 400 lb while that on the back increases to 368 lb, reducing the different to 32 lb.

Obviously this is something we should think about. When a rider weighing 128 lb sits on his horse in normal fashion 82 lb of his total weight is on the forelegs and 46 lb is carried on the hind legs. When he leans back, 20 lb is removed from the forelegs to the hind ones.

These figures not only show that neither the horse's own total weight nor the combined weight of horse and rider are evenly divided between fore and hind legs, but that the proportion is subject to change by a change of position of the horse's neck and head on one hand and that of the rider's body on the other.

These experiments were carried out with a standing horse on a two-scale balance. But the same weight transfers are obtained by variations in the degree to which the hind legs advance under the body. The weight division in two horses of exactly the same weight, for instance, standing with heads and necks in identical positions, is not divided up in the same way, if one is standing stretched out behind and the other is standing with his hind legs well under his body. Thus, if we take a horse with a normal leg formation (i.e. where a plumb line dropped from the point of the buttock meets the point of the hock, follows the cannon and then falls slightly behind the heel) and train him well enough to let us increase the engagement of the hind legs at will, we acquire a means to put more weight on the quarters and thereby lighten the forehand. We can also change the balance by combining this increased engagement of the hind legs with a raising of head and neck, so reducing the distance between these parts and the chest.

This combination is best, because with the horse halted straight the four legs, planted on the ground, form a rectangle called "the base of sustention" and the smaller this base the more sensitive is the existing balance to change, that is, it becomes easy for horse and rider to play with it, as it were, and the more quickly and smoothly will they be able to pass from movement to movement.

However, and this is fundamental, pursuit of a better, more sensitive balance must begin with the engagement of the hind legs. Raising the head and neck for *ramener** before this point has the most undesirable repercussions on unprepared quarters. Unfortunately, it is seen all too often because many riders rush to put the front end in what they consider a flattering position, without thinking about the quarters, and the result is usually to the detriment of this propulsive force.

And now a final reminder. Balance must be sought in conjunction with forward movement, the essence of equitation. Neither can be permitted to impair the other.

---

* *Ramener* is an attitude of the head produced by a flexion of the poll, allowed by the joints connecting the first cervical vertebra with the poll and second vertebra, and in which the poll remains the highest point in the overall carriage of the head and neck. In a complete *ramener* the face is held vertical and must not retreat behind this line so that the horse becomes 'overbent.' *Ramener* is produced by the advance of the body towards the head, not by a retraction of the head towards the body. The *ramener* is discussed in detail in the following chapter.

XXIII.
THE RAMENER

The term *head carriage* is loosely applied to both a natural and an acquired attitude, but it is incomplete because it does not include the very important participation of the neck. Therefore dressage experts keep using the French term *ramener*, which has been a part of equestrian terminology for as long as the concept itself has existed in equitation.

This *ramener* consists of a head position close to the vertical with the poll at the apex and is achieved by driving the body, and the neck, forward, the hands exerting a measure of opposition to this forward movement. This leads to a tightening of the angle formed by the first two cervical vertebrae and poll joints. The hand opposition must be so minimal and skillful, however, that it "filters" rather than blocks and, far from coercing the horse, causes him to yield willingly.

The *ramener*, let me repeat must be obtained, not by a retreat of the head towards the body, but *by the advance of the body towards the head*, the neck coiled in strict proportion to the extent to which the head is bent to the rear.

The pitfall for so many is that this near-vertical position of the head can, indeed, be obtained both ways, but the results are not at all alike. And yet it is the result that counts, because the *ramener* is not an end in itself but a means toward two ends. These are that it allows the bit to act with the greatest effectiveness on the lower jaw and it "tautens" the top line of the horse.

In obtaining *ramener* by a retreat of the head we should only be teaching the horse "to feel the bit," to pass behind it, whereas all training is directed towards teaching him to make contact with it. We want the horse to remain on the bit, even at the halt, yet not allow himself to be carried by it nor to pull against it. By forcing a retreat of the head we would prevent the essential engagement of the hind legs and in doing so prevent the "engine" from functioning properly. (This brings up the question of using side reins. Properly applied at a trot they may be useful in the hands of an experienced trainer who is able to see whether it is actually the hind legs that are driving the whole horse onto the bit. For the less experienced, however, this is something that is more easily felt from the saddle than seen from the ground.)

In seeking the *ramener* by an advance of the body toward the head, there are two dangers to avoid and a challenge to meet. If we try for *ramener* without the neck being at proper height the horse will overbend; and if we attempt to raise the neck without proper engagement of the hind legs, the base of the neck will cave in, resulting in the opposite of what we require. These are the dangers; the challenge lies in using your own good sense in the day-to-day work. No book can give you guidance on that score. No two horses are built the same way and you must recognize the limitations which may be imposed on your horse by his particular conformation.

The benefits of good *ramener*, obtained by classical means, extend over the entire horse and the finer, more sensitive balance to which it leads gives greater lightness, handiness, and more easily regulated flowing gaits. The accompanying engagement of the hind legs not only shortens the horse "at the bottom" but, also, from tail to poll, "at the top."

I mentioned, as one of the dangers attendant upon obtaining *ramener*, the caving in of the neck. Do not forget that whereas the hind legs are solidly attached to the spine the forelegs have no bony link with it, since the horse lacks a collar bone and the shoulders are held in place by nothing but muscles. If we try to raise the head excessively, the first cervical vertebra, close to the head, is pressed down and in turn presses down on the next one and so on down the line. This will result in a hollowing of the back and the hind legs, incapable of being engaged under the body, being dragged out behind. If, on the contrary, the lowering of the haunches comes about through a correct engagement the hind legs will push not only forward but upward. If this is combined with a *ramener* corresponding to the right neck ele-

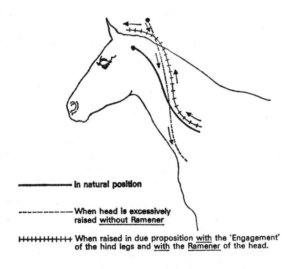

—————— In natural position

--------- When head is excessively raised without Ramener

++++++++++ When raised in due proposition with the 'Engagement' of the hind legs and with the Ramener of the head.

Fig. 2. *Ramener*. Sketch drawn from *Equitation Académique* by General Decarpentry.

vation, the cervical, and consequently all the dorsal and lumbar verte-brae, are stretched. (**See Fig. 2**).

With almost all young horses, though, and quite a few others, the neck and back muscles must be exercised before we can proceed to the *ramener*. The basic exercise for this is *neck stretching*, affecting not only the neck itself but the back and the hind legs, in fact, the entire animal, whose balance and gaits will be improved in consequence. The principle is simple: at the request of the rider the horse is asked to stretch his neck and head *forward and downward*. Yet it is a stretch with a difference!

Figures 3 (a) and 3 (b) show you not only the good and the extension, but also why they are good or bad. The way the horse stretches his neck by himself (**Fig. 3(a)**) is bad, because the hind legs do not drive, but just come bumbling after, making the base of the neck cave in. Any *ramener* using this position as a base can only be wrong. Yet if our leg action activates the hind legs they push the whole horse forward, en-gaging themselves under the mass all the more easily since the stretched and low position of neck and head gives the top line a convex shape (as in **Fig. 3(b)**). The exercise is, therefore, dependent on taut

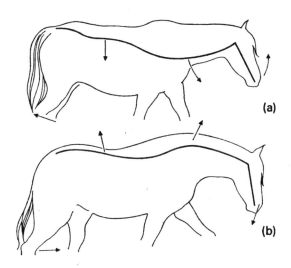

Fig. 3. Extension of the Neck. After a sketch by Major J. Licast. (a) *Natural Extension*: Hind legs *not engaged*, top line not rounded. Base of neck caved in. (b) *Extension requested*: Hind legs *engaged*, top line rounded. Base of neck raised.

reins, which keep the contact throughout the stretching, and on active legs which compel the quarters to become engaged.

But how do we obtain this neck stretching? Simply, by *combing the reins*, i.e. the hands being laid on the reins and sliding backwards alternately. Some of my pupils have found it comes more easily to the watching eyes than to the acting hands, so let me explain how it is done. We take both reins (always on the snaffle bit) near the base of the neck in the right hand, palm down, index finger separating them, the other fingers sufficiently closed to keep them tight. The exact tension and height are optional, but the finger closure must be soft enough to allow the hands to slide easily along the reins (which means that rubber or plaited reins are not practical). As the right hand gets to the end of its run, near our chest, the left takes over, taking hold of the reins at the same place and moving upwards in the same way. When this hand reaches the chest the other takes over and so on. As soon as the horse gives us the merest hint of stretching his neck our hand must yield sufficiently to allow it, without ever losing the permanent contact with the mouth. But all this can be effective only if our legs *act to engage the hind legs*.

This work, started at the walk, is continued at the rising trot at which gait it is most beneficial. Only after the neck muscles are developed and properly oriented may we quite safely tackle the *ramener*.

I have discussed *ramener* and how it is best obtained before describing the work involved in the half-turn on the haunches for a good reason. It is because this movement would lose most of its effect if the neck were extended and stretched more or less downward. Before it can be performed correctly *ramener* must have been obtained.

XXIV.
THE HALF-TURN ON THE HAUNCHES AND THE HALT

We have seen how the half-turn on the forehand teaches the horse to yield to the action of "the single leg" and we know that, as is the case with all other aids, the single leg can act, resist or yield. In the half-turn on the forehand it acted to mobilize the haunches now, in the half-turn on the haunches, it resists to keep them in place, a more delicate procedure.

In acting to shift the haunches, a somewhat stronger application of the leg would have caused no great harm; but when the leg resists to maintain the haunches, a force greater than the effort of the horse in trying to shift them in one direction will only result in their being moved in the opposite.

We begin the half-turn on the haunches after that on the forehand because:

(a) By teaching the forehand turn, involving a shift of the quarters from the action of the single leg, we have prepared the horse for the leg which resists an uncalled-for movement of the quarters. It follows that if he has learned to move away from the lightest pressure of a leg asking for a shift he will respond in like fashion to a resisting leg applied with the same intensity. It is only when we can shift his quarters at will that we are able, also, to resist any unwanted movement made by them.

(b) Most resistances on the part of the horse spring from the haunches, and, for a start, nothing dissolves them better than mobility.

(c) In the half-turn on the forehand at a walk the single leg has compelled the horse to engage the crossing hind, which now gives us the possibility of working either hind at will and so making their engagement as equal as can be. It is easier for the horse to have his hind legs suppled separately, which is something that we cannot do in the half-turn on the haunches.

The half-turn on the haunches does for the shoulders what the turn on the forehand did for the haunches; it gives them lateral mobility. It also rebalances the horse, whose equilibrium was necessarily affected during the half-turn on the forehand, since in any rotation of one end around the other the pivot end is burdened and the turning end lightened to the same extent. If this sounds too technical, think of yourself standing evenly on both feet and getting ready to turn left. To start with you must shift the weight from your right foot onto the left, which is going to be used as a pivot.

By practicing both these turning exercises with the horse it follows, providing they are done properly, that the overall balance will be improved. Let us consider, as an example, the half-turn on the haunches from right to left. The procedure for a turn to the opposite direction only involves your reversing the words "right" and "left."

We execute first, an ordinary half-volte on the track to the left, and then, at the very same spot, another smaller one, but still starting off from the track to the left. During the half-circle, the right leg slides back and obliges the haunches to remain on a track inside that made by the forelegs. A right counter-rein requests the shoulders to shift left. Under this action the horse will cross his forelegs, off passing in front of near, a crossing which at first will naturally be no more than minimal.

We make the half-voltes ever smaller, just as we used to do for the half-turn on the forehand, slowing the walk down before the counter-rein asks the shoulders for a lateral shift. This slow-down will be helped if we lean back a bit, and this will also cause us to put more weight on the quarters, which will make it more difficult for the quarters to shift sideways. On the other hand by putting more weight to the rear we shall have lightened the forehand correspondingly, allowing it to move sideways with greater freedom.

If we persist with the exercise, using the same aids, we shall eventually arrive at the half-turn on the haunches on the spot; and here, once more, the four limbs must throughout the movement maintain a regular walk, that is, the pivot leg (the *near* hind in this case) must execute the time proper to it, on the spot.

It is very important to perfect the half-turns at the walk before attempting them on the spot. The dangers in this movement are far greater than in the half-turn on the forehand where, unless we commit some outrageous error with our hand, there is little chance of the horse backing, since his quarters are in motion. In the turn on the forehand the most common fault is for the haunches to move out sideways because the hind leg, instead of passing over in front of its partner, only moves up to it without crossing. That is bad enough, but it is not nearly as bad as backward motion in the half-turn on the haunches.

If the reins are not taut enough in this movement the horse advances, which is wrong, but if they are too tight he retreats, which is worse. Therefore, the horse must have been carefully prepared for this exercise and the rider himself must have developed sufficient feeling to sense the point to which his hands can oppose the forward movement without causing the horse to back.

The classical aids for the half-turn on the haunches from right to left are as follows. We resist in the shoulders (by stretching the upper body) and draw them back very slightly in order to take some weight off the forehand and put it on the quarters, so preventing the hind legs from slipping out sideways. We use the right counter-rein (active aid) to drive the shoulders left; the right single leg (passive aid) keeps the haunches in place; the left leg at the girth maintains impulsion and so keeps the horse on the bit.

In concluding, let me stress the importance, common to both half-turns, of good timing, as it concerns the leg in the former instance and the hand (counter-rein) in the latter.

In either case we ask our horse to cross one leg, fore or hind, in front of the other, while all four beats of the walk remain clearly defined. Now, obviously, if we ask for a shift of the crossing leg just when the horse has it on the ground and is leaning on it he cannot move it. Further, if the determining leg or hand action ceases or diminishes considerably at the most propitious moment for the crossing, the horse will either fail to cross his legs altogether or will not be able to cross them sufficiently. If the active aids (single leg in one case, counter-rein in the other) are applied continuously and with unchanging intensity we will get the horse *falling* into the movement, the true gait will be lost and, to add insult to injury, the horse will finally snatch the movement from us, anticipating our request and leaving us impotent to stop it. So it is most important to vary our exercises as soon as the horse has learned to yield to the half-turn aids and so keep them from becoming routine. If we ask, for example, for a complete half-turn, step by step, then for just a couple of steps, followed perhaps by a walk on a straight line before we ask for another one or two steps the horse will never know how many steps he will be required to take at any one time and he cannot indulge in anticipation.

The improvement of even the simplest movement is long-term work, in which some progress may be expected daily but very little on any given day. Beware, above all, of using forcible aids, because the horse unfailingly responds to them by a much superior force of his own. Your physical strength is infinitely less then his, and at this kind of game the rider is always the loser. There is no way in which we can prevail over the horse except by mental education; and the better educated your horse is in this respect the more easily will he be able to cope with the difficulties that arise, within, of course, the limits of his physical capacity.

The Halt. In a dressage test the horse must halt straight, remain immobile and keep the contact on the bit. It sounds so very obvious that riders often do not realize just how difficult it is, and so we rarely see a good halt in a test. Yet judges pay particular attention to it because, in part, it is one of the movements which best reveals the quality of training.

Though this movement, as with all others, is not judged by identical standards in tests of different levels and its execution need not, in some of them, be perfect, it must be sufficiently correct to prove that classical principles have been followed in the horse's training.

Some of us are forever tackling feats for which neither we nor our horses are ready and which, in truth, are frequently not expected of us at the level we have reached. I am referring in particular to that overlightness of the mouth combined with a *ramener* which is way beyond our horses' training level. The result is a horse who, as soon as he is stopped, drops his bit, a serious fault by itself, and then makes matters worse by moving his head. He is then no longer "on the hand" and is, therefore, at least partially out of control. He is able to shift his legs and, worse of all, to evade contact and overbend.

Like all other movements, the halt is not judged in isolation but by the transitions connecting it with the preceding and following movements. If the horse has dropped his bit the restart into the forward movement can only be bad.

The two regions requiring our greatest attention here are the *back* and haunches plus the hind legs. The role of neck and head is secondary on our level, because they are quite passive. All we ask of them is not to do wrong, either by fighting the hand or by going up, a common fault with ewe-necked horses; and if I put most particular emphasis on the back, it is because one tends to forget about it. It is very rightly said that the horse does not travel solely with his four legs, but also with his back. If the back is weak, or poorly suppled, the forces issuing from the "engine" in the quarters are so badly transmitted to the forehand that its performance must be affected adversely.

If you are lucky enough to own a horse who halts correctly do not imagine for one moment that this has come about by itself; some blessed equestrian Kilroy has been there before you. And if you have a horse of the opposite inclination do not imagine that by repeating poor halts endlessly with this unprepared horse you will one day obtain good ones. He will never be able to give you a decent halt until his back and quarters have been suppled and developed for the movement.

Now let us see how this should be done. By work on the circle, plus serpentines and figure-eights, we first develop *lateral* suppleness and we straighten the horse by working longer and more often on the less satisfactory side. In these exercises the hind legs learn to engage themselves separately and once again we work more frequently on the less efficient leg by placing it on the inside of our circles, etc.

Once this work has borne fruit we proceed to develop *longitudinal* suppleness, where both hind legs must engage themselves simultaneously, and initially we do this by speed-ups and slow-downs of the gaits and by passing from walk to trot and back again, eventually including the canter pace.

By opening and closing the key joints of the quarters (sacro-iliac and coxo-femural) they are trained for the requirements of the halt where, after all, the chief and hardest task falls upon them. In speeding up and slowing down, and passing from one gait to another, the horse also learns to move forward freely at the prompting of the leg and to slow down at that of the hand.

If in the course of this work he has come to trust the hand he will not try to evade it in the arena, but will continue to keep a permanent contact on the bit. This is our first goal. Lightness of the mouth comes later, after he has understood that he must remain on the bit.

How do we request the halt? First, we ask for a slow-down of the current gait, commensurate with the horse's degree of training. In the highly schooled horse the slow-down will be virtually imperceptible, but we cannot expect this of a horse below that level. The purpose of this slow-down is twofold: it warns the horse of things to come and prepares him, physically, by a slight rebalancing toward the haunches which engages the hind legs. Our leg and hand aids at this moment must be smooth and gentle but at the same time clear and precise. Once the slow-down has been obtained we close the fingers of both hands, with our shoulders resisting, to obtain the halt, when we loosen our fingers slightly—in other words we yield because the horse has yielded.

During the halt the reins remain sufficiently taut for contact and the legs, also, remain in touch with the horse's sides.

Halting is usually followed by a period of "immobility," lasting from four to six seconds. The first rule here is for ourselves to remain immobile—often it is the little movement on our part that causes the horse to stir. Do not move anything, neither hands, nor fingers, neither legs not seat, not even your eyes. I don't mean to say that the act of blinking your eyes will, by itself, make the horse shift but if you fix them on some point you are less likely to make involuntary movements.

XXV.
THE REIN BACK AND REIN AIDS

In equitation we act alike for slowing down and reining back. The legs cease to request the forward movement but stay in contact, then they yield before the hands act alternately by a simple closing of the fingers over the reins. Never forget, however, that this closing of the fingers must be accompanied by a resistance in the shoulders with your elbows held close to the body. You must not, by advancing the elbows or the upper body, let your arms give what your hands are taking.

The fingerplay resembles the gentle squeezing of juice from two lemons, only it is much, much more gentle. Each hand, in its turn, closes without abruptness as the other opens, and they do so without sawing at the mouth. If you do this properly your horse's head will remain steady and not move from side to side, only the snaffle itself will glide softly over the mouth, making itself felt a little more first on one corner, then on the other. To this alternation of a mere increase and decrease of finger *pressures* the horse yields easily, while to simultaneous *traction* on both reins he will respond by an opposite and stronger traction of his own. Even if mentally he is still unwilling to yield, he finds it hard to resist for two reasons:

1. His fighting stance against the hand takes the form of a stiffened jaw, a "clenching of teeth." But the relaxing effect of this faint to and fro of the snaffle keeps the mouth soft.

2. To pull at the hand he needs a point to lean on, and the stronger and more solid this point the better he can pull at it. But this hold is refused him by our alternate use of the fingers of each hand under which the point of support can only occur momentarily before disappearing again.

If our legs and hands act in the way described at the ordinary trot, for instance, the horse will slow down the pace. If we persist, the trot will dwindle to its minimum speed and be followed by the walk which in turn will slow to a halt. If our hand action continues, then the horse will start into the rein back.

This is the theory, but the practical problem is somewhat more complex, because an easy, smooth rein back requires preparation and certain longitudinal suppling exercises, one of which happens to be the rein back itself. The main obstacles to a really good rein back are a hollow, feeble back, badly-coupled loins and nonengaged hind legs, the second fault usually being associated with the first. In fact nonengaged hind legs will, buttress-like, stem the retreating motions. But let us have a look at the actual technique of the rein back.

With a horse already trained to rein back the hands alternately exert finger pressures while the shoulders resist, the right hand prompting the retreat of the off diagonal, the left that of the near. The two crucial moments are the start into the rearward movement and the restart into forward motion.

The rein back from the halt after a few seconds' immobility is rarely required at the level we are discussing, but when it is we must be particularly careful about the halt. The horse must be kept engaged as well as on the bit, that is, he must be halted in good balance, which must not be lost during the period of immobility. So it is essential that we keep him well "framed" between our hands and legs throughout. Even when no immobility is required the halt must be well defined, but to make the rein back easier we reduce this static period to a minimum.

The intervention of the seat acquires considerable importance here. If we burrow into the saddle, leaning back a bit, the small of the back becomes blocked and this sort of action by the seat will hamper the rein back by being in opposition to the action of the hands. The upper body must remain straight and the seat supple if it is to feel the movement and follow it smoothly.

With a horse not yet trained to rein back it is simplest to start on foot, which is easier for us and the horse, who can comply without being bothered by our weight on his back.

We should face the horse's head, taking a snaffle ring in each hand and letting him place his head at his own height. We push him backward by alternate hand actions but if he will not go back we make him lower his head a little and then repeat the request with our hands while lightly stepping on his feet or pasterns. When he has yielded several times we return to mounted work where, to begin with, we lean more strongly on the stirrups during the movement rather than weighing down on his back and loins.

None of this normally causes too much trouble. The difficulties, indeed, are of a more subtle nature, the foremost of them being the problem of teaching the horse to *back his body while advancing with his mind.* It must be inculcated into the horse from the start that any backward movement is invariably followed by forward motion, a principle to keep in mind in the work in hand as well as in the saddle. Before we may even think of introducing him to the rein back we must be absolutely sure that free forward movement answers unquestioningly and instantly the action of the legs.

A past Chief Ecuyer at Saumur has given his prescription for the teaching of the rein back as "teaching the horse not to back." There is, indeed, a method which obtains the rein back by the legs driving the horse forward onto resisting hands—it is effective but risky for the rea-

son that it teaches the horse to go back in response to the same leg action which prompts him to go forward. Let us, for Heaven's sake, keep
the meaning of simultaneous leg action completely unequivocal: *free
forward movement* no more, no less. It must be preferable to a method
which involves the risk of confusing the horse in a matter where he
may be only too eager to misunderstand.

An added drawback to this last way of reining back is that it is not
possible to regulate the exact number of steps. The horse, pushed by
the legs, must, when he meets the resisting hand, rein back, so to
speak, on his own and we can then have little hope of controlling the
movement with any precision. And remember it is "precision" that
counts quite a lot with the dressage judge.

The Five Rein Effects

The opening rein (1st effect) has a natural action upon the horse.
It consists of drawing his nose in the direction one wants to take.
To turn right, make your right wrist pivot a quarter right turn,
thereby turning your nails up, and shift it to the right, keeping
your elbows close to the body.

The counter-rein (2nd effect), also called the neck rein, acts upon
the base of the neck which it nudges in the proposed direction. To
turn right, make your left wrist act from left to right and from
back to front. It is the only rein effect permitting you to manage
your horse with a single hand. Unlike the opening rein, the horse,
able to evade it without trouble, must be trained to obey it.

Both rein effects act on the forehand which takes the new direction, while the hindquarters are content to follow the shoulders in this change. Since the action does not interfere with the
forward movement, the horse does not tend to slow down.

By contrast the following three rein effects address the hindquarters. By a rational disposition of his reins, the rider opposes
the shoulders to the haunches, whence their appellation of reins
of opposition. This opposition impairs the forward movement
which the rider's legs must painstakingly keep intact or restore
whenever it tends to disappear; and the effectiveness of these
reins is commensurate with the degree of activity the rider creates in the hindquarters.

The direct rein of opposition acts upon the haunches and makes
the horse turn right by pushing his haunches to the left. In performing this rein effect, the rider tightens the right rein in the

direction of his right knee, after slightly relaxing the fingers of his left hand so as to make the horse understand more easily the action of the right. With this effect the reins remain parallel to the horse's axis.

The right counter-rein of opposition in front of the withers (4th effect) acts upon the shoulders and makes the horse turn left by throwing his shoulders to the left and his haunches to the right; the horse thus pivots around an axis passing approximately through the vertical of the stirrup leathers. In performing this rein effect, the rider, increasing finger pressure on the right rein, shifts his right wrist to the left, passing in front of the withers.

The right counter-rein of opposition passing behind the withers (5th effect or intermediate rein) acts upon the shoulders and the haunches and displaces the whole horse toward the left. This rein effect is intermediate between the direct rein of opposition, which only acts upon the haunches, and the counter-rein of opposition in

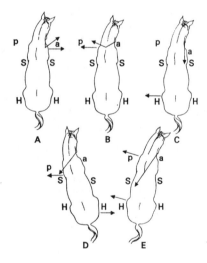

Fig. 4. The Five Rein Effects. (a) The opening rein; (b) The counter-rein; (c) The direct rein of opposition; (d) The right counter-rein of opposition in front of the withers; (e) The right counter-rein of opposition passing behind the withers.

The Coordination of the Aids and the Five Rein Effects

	Acting Rein	Forehand	Acting Leg	Hindquarters	New Direction Taken	Aids Applied
I.	Right opening rein	Drawn to the right	Right, pushing the haunches to the left, aiding the right turn.	Pushed to the left	To the right	Lateral*
II.	Right counter-rein	Pushed to the left	Left, pushing the haunches to the right, aiding the left turn.	Pushed to the right	To the left	Diagonal**
III.	Right direct rein of opposition	Turned to the right	Right, reinforcing the action of the right rein which pushes the haunches to the left.	Pushed to the left	To the right	Lateral
IV.	Right counter-rein of opposition in front of the withers; 4th effect	Pushed to the left	Left, reinforcing the action of the right rein which pushes the haunches to the right.	Pushed to the right	To the left	Diagonal
V.	Right counter-rein of opposition behind the withers; 5th effect or intermediate rein	Pushed to the left	Right, reinforcing the action of the right rein which pushes the haunches to the left.	Pushed to the left	The entire horse is lateral moved to the left.	Diagonal

* One calls lateral aids the combination of the hand and leg acting on the same side. Example: The right hand and leg are the right lateral aids.
** One calls diagonal aids the combination of the hand of one side and the leg of the opposite. Example: The left hand and right leg.

front of the withers, which only acts upon the shoulders. It thus falls to the rider, in shifting his right wrist towards the left, to determine how far behind the withers the right rein should pass in order to act with equal intensity upon shoulders and haunches; because the more this intermediate rein tends to approach the direct rein of opposition, the more it acts upon the hindquarters and, on the contrary, the more it tends to approach the counter-rein of opposition in front of the withers, the greater its effect on the forehand.

XXVI.
Changing Speeds and Gaits

This bogeyman of dressage tests should really cause no fear or trouble in the arena if the horse has been worked in the two types of suppling exercises, the lateral and longitudinal ones. Indeed, the latter consist of practically nothing but changes of speed and transitions between gaits.

The lateral suppling exercises are used to straighten the horse as much as possible, while the first longitudinal exercises work towards a lowering of the haunches and a consequent engagement of the hind legs. They increase the flexibility of the spine along its length and so develop the play of the sacro-iliac and coxo-femoral joints. Although eventually both exercises are practiced concurrently we work on lateral suppling first, because the joints affecting the spine usually flex better to the side than lengthways. Additionally, by tackling the more easily accomplished lateral suppleness first we make the longitudinal work, which follows, easier for our horse. It should be remembered that the horse cannot perform with any real precision in the longitudinal exercises until he is reasonably straight, and that is the purpose of lateral suppling.

Lateral Suppling

The principal exercise is the work on the circle, plus serpentines, figures of eight and the negotiating of corners. Though bones, of course, cannot be straightened it is possible, in the young horse, to create in the muscular system a dissymmetry to counteract that of the bones and thus, by compensation, to achieve a measure of straightness.

The principle of the work on the circle or on elements of curves relies on the combined use of both heels and both hands. On a right circle, for example, we use the right leading rein, operating the left rein to limit the bend of the neck and employing, if necessary, a counter-rein effect to push the shoulders to the right. The right leg, around which the horse is bending, is at the girth, while the left leg is held slightly back to maintain the haunches and keep them from slipping to the outside, that is, to the left. The theory is quite simple but its application is made more complex because the action of both hands and both legs, each reinforcing all the others, is subject to constant change.

As usual, we shall accomplish more by patient repetition than by hurrying the horse into making tight curves before he is physically capable of performing them. When he bends well on wide circles, and with equal ease to either side, we can then approach the longitudinal suppling period.

Longitudinal Suppling

This includes a mixture of speed-ups, slow-downs, changes of gait and finally the rein back, which we have already examined. Now let us see how these variations in the pace at specific gaits are best obtained.

We begin the work at the trot, a gait in which impulsion is greater and more easily preserved than at the walk. The canter, although lending itself to even more impulsion, has two drawbacks. First, the unsymmetrical form of the gait itself causes the horse to be unstraight and secondly its more exciting quality is a hazard to the necessary calm. So we use the trot, the rising trot, which relieves the horse's back, loins and, consequently, his hind legs of the weight they must bear with the rider at the sitting trot. It is necessary to rise to the trot since it is these parts which work hardest in the exercise.

As usual, do not expect too much at first. The hands yield clearly prior to the leg acting, and vice versa. In speeding up, the hands yield, then the legs are applied to produce a speed-up to the degree permitted by the hands. But his "yielding" of the hands and the time lapse between it and the leg action can vary infinitely. In the early stage, in order to prevent confusion in the horse's mind, the hands must yield completely and only keep a light contact with the mouth, the legs beginning to act only after the hands have yielded entirely. For slowing down the same precautions must be taken, the legs ceasing their action before the hands act.

Once the horse yields perfectly to these simple aids we go on to the next stage involving "resistance" of the hands in the speed-ups and of the legs in the slow-downs, without thereby losing their clarity as aids. Let us imagine that in speeding up the reins had a tension of *Intensity 10*. We yield to where this intensity dwindles to 3, but then our hands resist to conserve this *Intensity 3*, while our legs rise progressively from their own initial *Intensity 3* to *Intensity 10*. This is a different story from our early speed-ups, where rein tension was and remained at *Intensity 0*.

For the slow-down it is the same. The legs now yield but stay in contact at *Intensity 3*, while the hands act, progressively bringing rein tension from *Intensity 3* to *Intensity 10*. As our horse is making progress, the time lapse between leg and hand action dwindles, *without ever vanishing completely*.

When these speed-ups and slow-downs are performed well at the trot, they can be practiced at walk and canter. Still later in the training we pass from gait to gait: ordinary walk, slow walk, ordinary trot, strong trot, slow trot, extended walk, ordinary trot, ordinary canter, etc., until eventually we can include the rein back in these transitions and at the very end, the halt. It is in passing from rein back to walk, to trot, to canter, and back again, reducing to a minimum the dead time between the retrograde and forward movements, that we attain the height of longitudinal suppling.

XXVII.
THE CANTER

At this stage in our training program the work at the canter pursues two aims—easy departures into the gait and a straight horse at the strike-off and during the canter. Here, even more than elsewhere, it is a question of educating the horse's reflexes by psychological rather than physical means.

The means at our disposal are various, and their choice depends on a "diagnosis," much as one medicine will be efficacious in treating a certain disease while another will be necessary for a different ailment. If the physician errs in his diagnosis the remedy can, of course, turn out to be worse than the illness it was supposed to cure. The simile can be taken even further: one particular patient's reaction to an appropriate drug, for instance, may be so unfavorable that a change in the treatment will be required. Similarly, while we should use certain classical methods which will apply roughly to all horses, we must not allow ourselves to become inflexible towards the individual in our application of them.

Although the canter is dependent on mental education, it also relies upon balance. A favorable balance for the canter facilitates the mental education and, conversely, a good mental education helps to solve the problems of balance, because it predisposes the horse to seek his right balance at the strike-off.

To begin at the beginning we will take the case of a young horse. In the school we obtain the first canters by riding the rising trot on the *inside diagonal* (i.e. the rider sitting in the saddle as the left diagonal—left fore and right hind—comes to the ground on the circle left, and vice versa) and causing the horse to accelerate beyond the maximum trotting speed, with the result that he ends up by losing his balance and "falling" into the canter. We should attempt these first strike-offs into canter in the corner of the school where the turn will precipitate the loss of balance. When the horse has reached the point where he will "fall" into the canter on the "inside" lead on both reins we carry out the exercise outdoors using the same procedure, but without employing corners. We do not check to trot or walk too promptly but let him canter on for a few minutes with maximum freedom of neck, but without losing contact with the bit. If he goes too fast we slow him down by the voice, not the reins. This exercise is meant to let him find his cantering balance under our weight, and the various intonations of our voice should have acquired sufficient meaning for him during the first few weeks of lunging at walk and trot to give us the control we need. We must be careful to do just about an equal amount of work on both leads with merely a little extra practice being given to the lead he finds more difficult.

After some time we need no longer stay on straight lines but can request a few easy changes of direction on wide curves. After five or six weeks of this, with the rider remaining as passive as possible, we can return to lunging work, asking for departures at the canter from the trot and walk by using our voice assisted by the lunging whip. Concentrate at this point on giving the command at precisely the right moment until he canters on the word of command alone, without our having to use the whip. Once this can be obtained we mount again. Both legs must now act as evenly as possible and with equal intensity, just sufficient enough to impart the necessary impulsion which the hands will control. The actual strike-off into canter can be asked for by the voice, to which the horse is accustomed, and it is surprising how easily it will be obtained if the balance is fairly correct.

Now we must get such departures by our physical aids alone. For the left canter, the right leg slides slightly back and the left is held at the girth while the hands keep the horse's neck as straight as possible. At first the voice accompanies the aids but gradually we can dispense with its help. What is important is the double role of the outside leg: it signals to the horse that a departure on the inside lead is in the offing and at the same time prevents the haunches from being thrown to the outside, that is, into the position they would assume for the canter on the opposite lead. It is the inside leg which, acting at the girth with light pressures, actually prompts the canter.

If the outside leg action is too strong it will cause the horse to become crooked, particularly if his natural bend is to the left. This is the inherent bend of the canter, and when it occurs in this fashion the crookedness is that much more accentuated. Though we have no room in this outline to discuss the reasons for all these inflections there is no wishing them away and they are blatantly apparent to any judge in any test.

If your horse almost invariably strikes off into the left canter when your aids demand the right, use the wall to help you straighten him out. The root of the evil lies in the haunches dropping off to the left, a position conducive to the left canter. Therefore, track to the right and before applying the aids for the canter depart on the off lead, shift both wrists to the left while keeping the neck straight. In doing this, you place *the shoulders in front of the haunches*. The horse is then straight, or at least relatively so, and the haunches cannot escape to the left because the wall contains them far more efficaciously than could your left leg. There are several advantages to this procedure: first of all, you accustom your horse to striking off into the right canter straight, not crooked; secondly, your hand action, affecting the forehand, allows you to see the resulting position, while leg action, affecting the haunches, cannot be seen and you will not be able to judge the horse's overall position. Last, but not least, the rule in classical equitation is to straighten a horse by resetting the *shoulders in front of the haunches*, not vice versa.

Straightening the horse during the canter is even harder than at trot and walk and requires exercises well beyond our current scope and ability. What we must not do, however, in our first dressage tests is to aggravate the horse's bend by awkward aids. If you are on the left circle, for example, remember that your *outside* leg is to give nothing but a warning signal for the departure at the left canter, that it is, so to speak, a "position leg," not an "action leg." The acting leg, which prompts the departure, is the left one, which by being positioned at the girth cannot possibly cause the haunches to deviate. In this way your departures, even if they are not absolutely straight, will be correct by the standards of low-level dressage tests. Once the departure into canter has been obtained the outside leg remains slightly behind its normal place, but it is not used for impulsion. This remains the business of the inside leg which, because it is at the girth, is in no danger of tampering with the straightness of your horse. And while you are on the circle, remember that you use hand action to align shoulders with haunches, not leg action to align haunches with shoulders.

At the ordinary left canter you must "cadence" your gait by holding your left hand a little higher than the right, slightly opening and closing its fingers over the rein in rhythm with the movement. Act, indeed as though your hand had to permit each stride.

If you wish to slow down, resist with your shoulders and lengthen the time your fingers are closed so that your hand tells the horse, "Not so fast, slow down, wait for permission for the next stride." Conversely, if you want to push up to the strong canter lower this same hand, letting your fingers go almost limp. If the horse has been well trained, he ought to speed up of his own accord without needing increased leg action.

Establishing such understandings between horse and rider is a good policy; it prevents extreme responses due to insufficient or excessive leg action and, since the horse accelerates on his own, although with his rider's permission, the speed-ups are prompt but unhurried.

While training for this stronger canter, at first use the spurs at the moment when the yielding hand goes down. The horse will then quickly understand that he should accelerate as soon as the hand permits. This is a good example of educated reflexes making for a "vibrant" and "forward" horse.

The seat must, of course, follow the canter motion if you wish to maintain complete contact with your horse, but (and it is a big BUT) this movement should be limited to the seat itself and it should stop at the waist. Unless the upper body, primarily the shoulders, remains absolutely still your position becomes awkward and, which is worse, it gives the judges the impression that your horse is so sluggish to the legs that your seat must keep pushing for all it is worth. Don't push in this way, and when you have to check to the trot don't push at all, just follow the movement. If you push the horse lets the canter dwindle to and beyond its minimum speed, thus reaching the trot somewhere beyond the specified point. Alas, the adage "Better late than never" is not one that is appreciated by judges.

The Counter-Canter

Used at home for training, the counter-canter (employing the opposite lead, i.e. right lead on circle left, and vice versa) supples the horse, improves his balance and straightens his true canter to whatever degree this may be possible. In dressage tests it demonstrates the extent of suppleness and balance and the obedience to the aids. In either case, any forcible persuasion, however slight, is wrong. In training because it would make us lose the benefits accruing from the exercise and during a test because it would cost us marks. Coercion in the execution of the counter-canter is particularly obvious because it is one of the movements where, even if we camouflage certain actions of our own, we cannot camouflage the horse's reactions to them. Judges tend to be all the more severe in these cases because in itself the counter-canter is not difficult. Though some call the counter-canter "unnatural" and purposeless it is not so, being the natural complement of the other work at the canter.

We only need look at horses cantering spontaneously at liberty to see that, aside from a very few who are "ambidextrous," most will favor a given leg and when there is sufficient space will gaily negotiate turns on their favorite lead, even though it be a false canter, changing only if their balance is jeopardized by the speed of their approach. To be honest, however, it is not this false canter we are looking for. In dressage tests the horse is expected to counter-canter on either lead, not as he does at liberty to canter on the lead he is more comfortable on. So our training aim is to render him equally skillful on both leads.

The progression leading to counter-canter is as follows. Once the general training has reached a point where we can control our horse without forcible aids of any sort we ride him in long canters at the speed most comfortable to him; accustoming him to cantering as easily on one lead as on the other but working longer and more often on the problem lead. When the departures at the canter are as easy to obtain on one lead as on the other, when we feel the back muscles are relaxed under our seat and the movement is quite effortless and supple, then, and only then, can we begin to introduce the counter-canter. It is better to start the exercise outside where walls and turns do not compel us to take one direction when it might be better for the horse's education to take another.

Riding on the left lead, on a barely perceptible curve, we first ask for change of direction to the right, then to the left, and then again to the right. We should not intensify the aids at the moment of change to the right but if we feel him about to become disunited or in danger of changing his leading leg we must turn to the left rather than put him off balance and interrupt the smoothness of the gait. If, as happens at times, we cannot prevent a change of lead or a disunited canter we must check to the walk and depart in canter on the same lead at the very spot where the mishap occurred. No punishment can be contemplated at this stage.

We do this every day, tightening, as progress allows, the curves at the counter-canter to the point required in the tests for which we are preparing. The hands are the sole aids in the various changes of direction, the legs doing no more than to preserve and maintain impulsion, being used simultaneously and with an absolutely even pressure. If one leg is stronger than the other we risk interfering with the gait and prompting a change of lead. The right counter-rein effects the left turn on the near lead, the right direct rein of opposition the right turn at the left counter-canter and, of course, vice versa. Be careful to keep the seat still; if it is allowed to shift the horse can easily become confused.

These are the secrets of the counter-canter but in the last analysis it is a question of the rider giving the utmost liberty to the horse while he himself, beyond giving minimal directives, remains passive. Ridden in this way the horse will not stiffen up during the performance which would be a sure sign that he was fighting his rider. All that is really required of the latter is an ability to feel whether or not his horse is ready to give what is about to be asked. It is the kind of "feel for the horse" which is essentially the art of horsemanship.

One particular problem in the counter-canter is perhaps the general canter problem of neck inflection. Ideally, the horse should be straight, but this standard is not required at the level we are discussing. A slight inflection to the side of the lead is allowable, because in giving the horse a certain necessary balance it allows and helps him to hold his canter and prevents his making an ill-timed change. In addition it makes the weight flow back to the opposite shoulder, thus lightening the shoulder on the lead-side, a very welcome occurrence at a moment when we wish to help the lead-side and hold back the other.

XXVIII.
THE SECOND AND THIRD COMMANDMENTS

Impulsion is an important point under the heading GENERAL IMPRESSIONS on the score sheet. Consciously or otherwise, the judges' marks in this respect are a compound of the impulsion, or lack of it, underlying each single movement. Since none of these can be quite correct without sufficient impulsion you may be sure that if there are a dozen movements in the test the final mark on the score sheet is the sum total of a dozen mental notes. But what is impulsion? In the first place, although people tend to use the two terms interchangeably, impulsion is not the same as forward movement. Forward movement is a physical motion, impulsion is a moral quality. A horse can advance at walk, trot or canter without an ounce of impulsion being present. Conversely, in the *piaffe*, for instance, which requires impulsion without advance, he trots on the spot, yet is ready and eager to go forward at the slightest prompting. The hallmark of impulsion is to be found in the really well-trained horse who will even rein back under impulsion.

The most apt of the many metaphors which seek to define impulsion as distinct from forward movement seems to be that of the steam boiler, which generates energy (forward movement) only if the steam (impulsion) can be channeled through a controlling valve (the hands). All horses have, in varying degrees, some natural impulsion and it is the development and control of this quality which is a principle aim in training.

With few exceptions forward movement is obtained by legs alone, but impulsion requires legs plus hands, the two acting alternately and never simultaneously. The legs create and/or increase the impulsion; the hands either store it or allow it to transform itself into speed.

You will remember that the trainer's *first commandment* prescribes calm. Once the young horse, by acquiring calmness, has come to trust the trainer, the *second commandment—forward*—occupies the trainer's attention. The horse is worked on the lunge line and with the lunging whip. Gradually as the horse learns to associate the whip and click of the tongue we proceed, possibly after some weeks, to mounted work, in order to get the horse to understand the meaning of leg action. Once more, the best and simplest means to employ with the young horse is to get him to associate a request to go forward with the whip rather than the spurs; and this is just as valid for your trained horse. Whenever you have trouble with the forward movement the sting of the whip is a more effective incitement than the prick of the spur.

Holding both reins evenly in a single hand, your legs request the forward movement and are followed up instantly by a whiplash just behind your leg. Your horse will almost certainly bound forward! Let him do so and pat him immediately. Do not rein in too soon but let him canter a good hundred yards before gently calming him by voice to a slow-down. After a few minutes' rest, on long reins, repeat the exercise, then send him back to the stables. I lay any odds that at your next ride he will spring forward at the slightest prompting of your legs.

It is a simple recipe within the means of any rider, but, as is the case with any recipe, the final quality of the dish depends on the quality of the ingredients. So remember the order in which the aids are applied. The leg action must be clearly defined but not too strong; the rein hand must advance sufficiently for it to ensure that the horse meets no resistance when he bounds forward; finally, the whiplash must come down energetically a split second after the leg action, without waiting for any reaction to the leg signal. As soon as the horse moves forward vigorously, pat him, without waiting for slow-down to the walk. You should, incidentally, be quite sure that your seat is sufficiently strong to keep you in the saddle no matter how violent your student's reaction to this "lesson of the legs." If you can't stay with him you teach the horse the quite counter-productive lesson that you can be shaken off, open entirely new horizons to his innocence and tell him what to do with a cumbersome and annoying weight on his back. This lesson of the legs should be given several times whenever the horse seems to be getting unresponsive to their use.

So far so good, but what if the hands keep destroying what the legs have so painstakingly wrought? Not only will the entire work have to be redone but after a few repeated mistakes by the hand your horse will become fed up with the whole affair. It is then your fault. You have dulled his spirit just as a carefully sharpened knife of fine steel will soon be dulled if used to chop wood. Resharpened it will cut again, but too many sharpenings whittle away the blade. So let your hands be, remain light, content to "indicate"—no more. In any disagreement with your horse, have recourse to your legs and tone down the effect of your hands. Three-quarters of all resistances are caused by the hands—hands that are too hard. Keeping your horse ever fresh to the legs, ever keen to advance, will avoid all kinds of trouble.

As for the *third commandment*, the degree of *straightness* necessary in dressage depends on the standard of the test and nowhere on your score sheet will you find the actual word spelled out. Yet straightness, or the lack of it, has profound repercussions on the *gaits*, on lightness and on the ease shown in the execution of the movements.

To many a straight horse is the one whose haunches, in following a straight line, do not fall to right or left and do not shift. This is nothing less than the truth, but it is not all of it.

Admittedly, the horse is not naturally straight, any more than you and I. In fact, only three out of a thousand human beings have a perfectly straight spine. Lack of straightness in the horse is due to the fact that one side is convex and the other, usually the near side, is concave. This natural bend in the horse is aggravated by our own habits. By approaching, bridling, saddling and leading from the near side we get him into the habit of looking left more often than right. Except for the south-paws among us, we tend to lunge him more often to the left, and, also, if you have been around riding schools, you may have noticed that more often than not all the riders are on the left rein and that they stay on it longer than they do on the right.

Furthermore, horses themselves are seldom ambidextrous. They prefer to canter on the near lead, they perform the half-pass more easily from right to left and do half-turns on the forehand better when the haunches are driven to the left, and so on. If we do not watch out for this from the beginning this additional factor, leading to greater crookedness, gets worse and worse.

To give an example: a rider who is more comfortable on the off diagonal, trots longer on it than on the other up to the point where the horse himself takes to casting him back onto the habitual diagonal, should the rider ever manage to get on the opposite one, by putting in a false beat. Since this gets worse with time, routine and age we should when buying an already trained or partly trained horse be particularly careful to pick one that is straight or almost so.

Actually, a horse is really straight when, following a straight course, the line of his spine (from poll to tail) corresponds with the line of travel, with both lateral pairs of legs being carried equally on either side of this line. The same is true when following a curve, when the bend of not only the neck but of the entire body is even and harmonious and each hind leg touches down on the track of the corresponding fore. Once this is so haunches and shoulders are so placed as to assure the straightness of their relative movement, weight distribution is regular, the forces of quarters and forehand harmonize, resistance vanishes and the horse is light.

The Three Commandments—*calm*, *forward* and *straight*—must be ever foremost in your mind, whatever the movement you are working on. All three are equally important, but the order of enforcement calls for calm first, and this calm, unlike the other two requisites, must be complete in any kind of riding. Then comes the forward movement, without which we could not make use of, and control, the impulsive forces which are destined to become an instrument in straightening the horse.

XXIX.
WORK ON TWO TRACKS

Two-track work, which comprises several movements, derives its name from the fact that the fore and hind legs follow different tracks, while in one-track work both follow the same. To save misunderstandings let us make it clear that neither term should be taken literally. In reality, one-track work, where the hind follow the forelegs in perfectly straight alignment, produces two tracks, one for each lateral pair of legs. Half-pass and shoulder-in, the principal two-track exercises, really produce four tracks, one for each leg.

In *shoulder-in* the horse is bent, traveling sideways yet always forward in the direction of his convex side. The legs of the concave (near side in the left shoulder-in) cross in front of those of the convex side. The *half-pass*, in its classical form, has the horse straight (rectilineal) from head to dock, except for a slight bend of the head in the direction of the movement (left in the left half-pass). This bend of the head should be sufficient just to let the rider see the corner of the eye on the inflected side. For all its slightness, this bend has a repercussion on the entire spine, causing it to take on an even less perceptible bend which adds to the horse's grace and helps to draw along the outside shoulder. It is the outside shoulder, of course, which does most of the work.

In both movements the main pitfall is an easily detectable loss of impulsion, since the horse noticeably slows down just as he goes from one-track into two-track motion. Remember, here as elsewhere, good impulsion is basic! Another rule to remember is that the crossed leg regulates the work of the crossing one in the half-pass.

What actual purpose has the work on two tracks? Well, most particularly, it supples and strengthens the dorsal and lumbar muscles, by causing them to play in an unusual direction. It also lightens the forehand and engages the hind legs, so improving balance and making the horse more agile, and, as well, it gives him the ability to change this balance effortlessly.

And what kind of progression should we follow? Let me say first of all that we should not even start one before the horse can yield easily to the single leg shifting the haunches. To teach him to cross his hind legs correctly we have already practiced half-voltes in reverse, shifting the haunches, and we have reached the point where in half-voltes, holding the haunches with the leg, we can shift the shoulders by a counter-rein so that the forelegs cross while advancing in the same way as the hind legs do in the half-voltes in reverse. As I explained, this led naturally into the half-turns on forehand and haunches. In other words, we should at this stage be able to obtain half-passes, independently so to speak, from both fore and hind legs. The problem we now have is "to put both ends together."

Not only have we obtained this lateral mobility of forehand and quarters with the legs crossing, but we have also taught the horse to bend in exercises on the circle, which is so important in obtaining a true half-pass. In the half-pass to the left, for example, the head is bent to the left and the horse moves left and FORWARD, the off fore and off hind crossing in front of the near legs. But we must appreciate that the further the near hind advances under the body the greater is the strain imposed on the off hind in making the crossover. If the horse avoids making this effort he will hold back with his near hind and move it sideways. This will cause a considerable loss of forward movement, since the release of the near hind no longer drives him sufficiently ahead and in this instance the improvement in engagement expected from the work on two tracks will not be realized. But the work on the circle has taught the horse to engage his inside hind which thus supports the mass and we are now able to control this engagement with our inside leg at the girth. Just as half-voltes and half-voltes in reverse were at the root of the crossing work, so the work on the circle is at the root of the engagement of the inside hind.

So we can begin the two-track work properly by using the shoulder-in, the horse's ultimate preparation for the half-pass. We work in this order because the end of the horse's whole body and the direction he follows in the shoulder-in puts a greater crossing strain on the forelegs which in any case experience more difficulty in crossing than the hind. Additionally, the aids for shoulder-in are easier from the rider's viewpoint than those for the half-pass.

The Two-Track Movements

Shoulder-in. In the shoulder-in the horse must be *uniformly* bent from head to dock to one side while moving forward in the opposite direction. This inward curve must initially be extremely slight, but it must be even throughout the horse's length and the tracks made by the fore and hind legs must be quite distinct. Too often we see excessively curved necks with almost straight bodies, with the result that we get a "broken" base to the neck which frustrates any effect of the "active" rein on the quarters.

The application of the aids for, let us say, the left shoulder-in is as follows: The left counter-rein of opposition passing behind the withers shifts shoulders and haunches to the right equally, if, of course, the hand is properly placed; the horse is then bent to the left. In order to limit the inflection given to the neck by this left rein, *the right hand*, after yielding, resists to maintain the required degree of inflection. *The right leg*, slightly behind its normal place, keeps the rightward shift of the haunches from becoming exaggerated, then it yields as needed when the haunches remain in position and in the correct relation to the overall inflection. The leg resists to oppose any excessive movement to the right which threatens to change the inflection. The primary purpose of the left leg is to maintain impulsion while, incidentally, reinforcing the action of the left rein by driving the haunches to the right.

In dressage tests the rider begins and ends the shoulder-in at a given spot, starting from either a straight or a curved line. In training, however, it is preferable to start from the circle for two important reasons. First, it lets us bend the horse in accordance with the chosen curve—the wider the circle, the less the bend—and secondly, it gives us plenty of time to prepare him. Actually, if the horse is still not ready after one circle there is nothing to prevent us from riding a second one at the same place. Besides this, when we return to ordinary one-track motion on the straight line after a few steps of shoulder-in (three or four at most in the early phase) the bend is lost and the horse has to be prepared all over again for the next few steps. When we want to stop the shoulder-in we keep the bend, using a circle as the base, and simply drive the horse forward on the circle which we have already begun.

Here is what happens when we put the horse into the left shoulder-in. On the track to the left, we describe a wide left-handed circle to obtain a slight overall bend from poll to tail and we keep riding the circle until the horse has achieved the bend we want and is correctly positioned for the movement. Once he is moving in this proper bend we request the shoulder-in by applying the left counter-rein of opposition passing behind the withers at the precise moment when the forelegs are leaving the track, and while the hind legs are still on it. We execute three, four, five steps of shoulder-in, then put the horse forward again by ceasing the left rein action and pushing him ahead on the circle which we have already started. We can then repeat the exercise as we wish.

I hope I have now made it clear that during the entire period, whether we are on one or two tracks, the horse remains in the same bend, so that the exercise may be continued or discontinued quite easily at any moment. Setting off from a straight line instead of from a circle makes it necessary for us to put the horse in the correct bend in a split second. This is always difficult to accomplish successfully and with a young horse it is really impossible. Then, of course, when operating from the straight line we must inevitably, as we return to it, lose the bend and be forced to request it again the next time we want our few steps at shoulder-in.

This bend, the proper poll to tail bend, is the essence of the shoulder-in and it is more important in the early stages than even the extent to which the legs cross. With practice the correct and full crossing of the legs can be easily enough developed.

Half-Pass

By exercising the horse in oblique travel in the shoulder-in we make him agile and obedient to reins and heels. Having reached this point we can then introduce the half-pass. Once more, the extent to which the horse is inclined obliquely must at first be minimal and must never exceed 30–40 degrees or, at the very outside, 45 degrees.

One can begin by the head to the wall exercise but, while this helps us judge the exact degree of obliquity and lets us use the wall to hold the horse's legs on the respective tracks, it has the drawback of encouraging the horse to slow down when starting into the half-pass. It is much better to begin by riding the half-volte, holding the haunches with the legs and returning to the track by two or three steps of the half-pass. Far from detracting from the forward movement the return to the track, in fact, is a means of promoting it. The half-volte also, and most usefully, prevents us from making any excessive demand.

The aids for the half-pass to the left are as follows. *Right counter-rein*, to drive the shoulders to the left, *right leg*, held slightly back, to drive the haunches to the left, *left rein* giving the head inflection to the left and regulating the gait in coordination with the right. The *left leg* maintains impulsion and watches over the engagement of the near-hind and the *body weight* is placed more upon the left buttock and stirrup.

After this exercise on the half-volte we can, indeed, go on to head to the wall, and when this is done correctly and easily we can make a further improvement by employing tail to the wall, so that the wall no longer guides us or our horse and our aids alone keep the legs on their respective tracks.

Still later comes the half-pass on the diagonal, in which the dangers of anticipation can so easily arise. The haunches can either laterally anticipate the shoulders and/or the horse himself can anticipate the movement and even take charge of it. The last may be avoided by never half-passing the full length of the diagonal and never requesting the same number of steps twice in succession. We might begin the half-pass, for instance, coming out of the corner, execute three or four steps, walk straight for a varying number of steps, continue the half-pass in the same direction for two more steps and then once more walk straight. In this way the horse is obliged to be ever alert to the aids and he never dares anticipate.

The last phase of half-pass work consists of counter-changes of hand, which are nothing but a combination of a half-pass in one direction followed, without a transitional break, by another to the opposite side. Since the previous work, progressively reducing the direct travel between half-passes, has rendered the horse obedient and light to legs and hand he should be capable of swift changes of balance on his own. All we need do to accomplish counter-change of hand is to straighten our horse completely during the last half-pass step and start into the first step of the half-pass in the opposite direction by first driving the shoulders in the new direction. We would do well for now to refrain from intervening with the leg in charge of driving the haunches, lest it cause them to precede the shoulders, which is a very serious fault!

XXX.
GENERAL IMPRESSIONS

Most of you will have had some show experience prior to entering dressage or combined training tests. In show-jumping competitions you expect the horse to make a somewhat greater effort on the day of competition than during training sessions. After all, it is only a matter of a little more of the same stuff, the fences being a little higher here and a little wider there. In fact, each successive show is really part of the training progression.

But this is not the case in the dressage test, which probes not so much *what* your horse has learned to do but *how* he has learned to do it and with how much ease, suppleness, lightness and freedom. These four points are indeed among those on the score sheet under GENERAL IMPRESSIONS and you will always get better marks if you take the horse to the standard of test where, rather than having to ask him for a little more than in everyday work, you can ask him for a little less than he is really capable of producing.

In show-jumping there were two ways of making time: first by not losing any, then by gaining some. In dressage tests, too, there are important omissions and commissions, errors easy to avoid and finishing touches to work out prior to presentation. Some of them are small points but, nevertheless, they can make the difference between success and failure.

Dressage riders would learn a lot if they had a chance to watch a test from the judge's seat. They would then see the movements from a different angle and better understand the importance of certain details. From his vantage point the judge can see the whole arena: four sides, four straight angles, the letters dividing it and the center line running in front of his seat. Everything is straight and perfectly visible on this carefully prepared piece of ground on which you, the competitor, have to ride. You make your entrance on the center line, coming to a halt at X, saluting the judge and departing to begin your test from this exact and conspicuous point in the empty rectangle. Have you ever thought that the judge's attitude for the next few minutes will be conditioned favorably or otherwise, by this arrival, halt and departure from X?

Too many of you act as though these three simple (but not easy) movements were not an integral part of the test. There is a certain *laisser-aller* about this part of the test; the horse does not arrive straight, he halts on the installment plan and not with any noticeable straightness either and he ambles off again as though it really didn't matter. The judge may not mark this first movement too severely, it is true, unless it actually approaches the above extreme, but you have alerted him to what might follow and at the very first fault the blow will fall.

As you enter at the trot or canter you must give the judge the impression that you have the situation and your horse both well in hand. "Give the impression" does not mean "bluff;" the self-assurance must be real, but it must, also, be apparent. Aside from the psychological effect on the judge, the movements will be more correct, the horse will obey your aids better and your adherence to the requirements of the test will be far superior. In sum, while you should not be a show-off, your bearing on horseback should be a show-off's dream. Other items listed under GEN-ERAL IMPRESSIONS on the score sheet are *position* and *aids*.

The position, which we have already discussed, must be classical. It must give the appearance of being utterly habitual and infinitely comfortable. Indeed not only must it look so but it must *be* so if you want to do your test precisely and smoothly.

Watch your head: look high and far ahead when on a straight line; in changing direction look at the point where you want to go before letting your hands and legs act, and on a circle do not forget to advance your outside shoulder a bit to keep facing the direction in which you are going, so that you are not left behind the horse's movement.

Your use of aids should be correct, that is, efficacious, accurate and discreet. If they fulfill all three requirements the judge will recognize them as the fruit of long and patient homework and good training of both rider and horse, that has resulted in an obvious mutual trust. Any improvisation during the test, however brilliant, only serves to produce confusion and disorder.

Watch your legs: they usually move too much. "Rocked" by the cadence of the trot they can give the impression that you *must* push your mount incessantly. If, in fact, you really have to push him, do so by lively but brief actions, making sure they are not so lively that he jumps out of his skin.

Let me give you an additional tip which you can make use of when you are in certain parts of the arena. Since the judge sits behind letter C, if you are on the right rein, say, between B–A–C, it follows that it is impossible for him to see your left leg, but he has a jolly good view of the right one. Therefore, keep the right leg still and use the left! It takes reasonable tact, of course, to prevent the horse from giving you away, since if your action is too strong he is prone to let the cat out of the bag.

If your aids are to be discreet without loss of efficacy you must learn to "prepare" your horse in good time. The more accurately you are able to choose the right moment and the right manner for this preparation the better the movement to follow will be, the more easily will it be obtained and the more natural will be the ultimate execution. Except in the case of an insufficiently trained or a highly-strung horse, loss of calm is caused by the horse being "surprised" by the aids.

If you shout the command "Quick March" at a squad of soldiers standing "at ease" the result will be chaotic. If you prepare them for the order by first bringing them to attention and then giving them a preliminary warning of the command which is to follow they will move off smoothly and precisely. It is exactly the same with the horse.

The Art of Passing and Accepting Judgment

Schooling a horse for dressage tests requires daily work over a prolonged period and is probably less enjoyable than sailing over fences when training a jumper. Aspiring dressage riders, commendably and necessarily, do not mind this painstaking preparation, but their one horror seems to be the actual riding of the test. I think, perhaps, it is the dread of the unknown, of the intangible. Unlike show-jumping or cross-country, where the faults incurred are entirely incontestible, the dressage arena cannot reveal faults in this way. Marks depend on the quality, or lack of it, in executing a series of movements and this is something which cannot approach the "black and white" of the dislodged pole or the deliberate refusal. It is sometimes very difficult for a rider to understand the mark for a particular movement, but if you tend to feel sorry for yourself and hard done by let me assure you that it is not all plain sailing for the judge either. Even in the great international competitions, where he can comfortably score on the basis of a firm standard of "perfection," defined for him by the rules of the Fédération Equestre Internationale, we find differences, usually negligible but sometimes not, in the scoring of three judges. Though this situation is definitely open to improvement, absolute agreement is probably impossible on this earth, since two, let alone three, people will never feel exactly the same way about anything. There is also the long period of time over which total concentration is required of the judges if they are to observe every movement made by the horse and rider with equal thoroughness. Naturally the capacity for prolonged concentration will vary from one judge to another, although all should possess it to an acceptable degree.

In the official FEI test for the Three-Day Event, where certain movements must be performed at the collected trot, there is no indication which would help the judges to determine the degree of collection required, though it is obvious that it is not meant to be the equal of that required in the Grand Prix de Dressage. In tests at a lower level things become even more complicated for the judge. He no longer has "absolute" perfection for his yardstick in anything, but is left with nothing more precise than a "relative" perfection, theoretically dictated by the test level itself but in practice largely left to his own interpretation. His actual base, in fact, is pathetically fluid.

Take a test of medium difficulty performed by twenty riders. The judge knows the standard of the test, but not of the riders and horses. Some of them are sure to be very good, some will be pretty bad, and the majority will be of medium standard. This state of affairs is bound to be reflected in his scoring, and usually is. Suppose his marks for the first entries are either fairly high or fairly low, how far up or down will this initial judgment push his marks as better or worse riders come onto the scene?

I know that this predicament could be avoided by using the same judge, who knows most of the horses and riders, time after time. But then again, we find ourselves between the devil and the deep blue sea, because this judge, scrupulously objective though he may be, is human, not a robot, and he cannot entirely rid his subconscious mind of past impressions.

Anyway, in practice it is nearly impossible to secure such continuity, even if it were desirable. Normally the judge is unfamiliar with contestants and horses and must play it by ear as the first three or four riders perform, waiting to gain a general impression of the true level of the class he is judging. Then, if the general execution of a movement (such as departures at the canter, counter-canter work, halts, rein backs, etc.) happens to be fair to middling, but good in one or two cases, he will tend to score these two performances a little higher than is warranted by their actual quality. Those two fortunates will score a 9 or even 10 but they should not be deluded by this very relative mark into believing that the movement in question is no longer subject to improvement.

Hence, judges' marks must be interpreted bearing in mind their double meaning—the value of the movement within the context of the test and within that of the group performing it. For these reasons we can gain only a very tentative notion of the true value of a performance by comparing two or three score sheets of equivalent tests ridden at different venues and under different judges.

For international tests we have a relatively small list of judges, and when members of such a panel arrive at an event they usually know each other and can discuss, if they have not done so in the past, their respective points of view and ways of judging certain movements, and so some common guidelines can be established. In local competitions this is impossible, at least in practice, which is a pity; for it would be most desirable in the elementary tests to have a panel of first-rate judges who could set the young riders onto the right track from the start.

I grant you that judges are not always perfect but perhaps the day will come when we shall have official examinations recognizing only truly qualified judges. By doing so we may then be able to produce unity in the manner of training and riding and a correspondingly uniform system of judging and scoring. But even then do not expect judges, any more than riders, to become infallible. Involuntary lapses on both side are bound to occur. Some movements come in swift sequels and must be scored very rapidly, requiring the practiced, keen eye, the "judging reflexes," in fact, which are the mirror of the "riding reflexes" you, on the other side of the white fence, must learn to develop.

There is a further contribution that the judges could make right now to help competitors. Aside from jotting down their scores and a few observations in the space reserved for such remarks, they should not only be available to answer questions after the test, but should take the initiative in explaining their judgments; commenting on the individual tests, underscoring what was best and what was worst; pointing out the causes of shortcomings and advising on the means to remedy them. The reasonable rider will not mind a measure of harsh criticism, as long as it is constructive, and only by this method will the true purpose of the dressage test, as an aid towards perfection, be served.

Of course it is nice to be first, and it is natural and right that this should be the objective, but there is more than this in competition. Whatever our final position, we should not forget that we enter tests to get an evaluation of our homework, a measuring of our progress. Thus the dressage test is both an end and a means.

But even the color of our rosettes may be somewhat misleading. I am the first to say that "it is a poor workman who always blames his tool," but there is not the slightest doubt that some horses make it easier to win on than others. If you are able to improve a rather unpromising horse to the point of being placed near the top of a given test you are more than likely to reach first place when given a chance to ride a better one.

I have wanted to explain these points in order to put into perspective the discouragement which I know can lurk in the four corners of dressage arenas and can so easily affect the young competitor. A famous judge and examiner whom I knew well used to say: "I'll give you twenty-four hours after the test to curse your judges, but then get back to work." If you want to make progress, be persevering, open to criticism and wary of praise.

Index

A

acting operations, 15, 16, 54,
137–138
aids. *See also* hands; legs; weight
distribution
overview, 15–16
active, 143–144
body weight as, 19–20
classifications of, 15, 143
coordination of, 20, 137, 141,
142, 144–145, 173
diagonal, 111, 147, 154–155
dressage tests and, 196–197
forcible, using, 165
forward movement, 186
as language, 2
lateral, 147–148
mind, xx
passive, 143
placer, 67
rein effects and, 173
seat, 136, 140–141, 181–182
for suppling exercises, 176
voice, 6, 180
ambidexterity, 182, 187
*"A New Method and Extraordinary
Invention to Dress Horses and
Work them According to Nature
by the Subtlety of Art"*
(Cavendish), xvii, 129
Aure, Count d', 122, 152

B

back, horse's, 166
backward movement. *See* rein
back
balance
canter and counter-canter for,
179, 182
improvement of, 164
in longitudinal suppling, 84
pace development and, 52

in piaffe, 119
weight distribution and, 21–28,
50, 157–158
base of sustention, 158
basse-école, 129
Baucher, François, 20, 21–23,
122–123
Baucher snaffles, 11, 12, 47
bending, 75–81, 189
Berlin Horse Show of 1936, 124
bits, 11–13, 139–140, 159
bodily harmony, 1–2, 130–132, 166
body weight, 19–20
breaking in, 129
bridles, 11–14
buttocks, rider's, 136, 140–141,
181–182

C

Cadre Noir (Saumur), 122, 124, 137
Calm, Forward, Straight, 3, 149,
185, 187
calmness, 53–54, 149–150, 187
canter. *See also* counter-canter
for balance, 179, 182
departures at, 85–88, 103–104,
179–181
in early training, 73
placer for, 103
suppling exercises with,
176, 177
Cavalry School (Saumur), 122,
124, 137
Cavendish, William, Duke of
Newcastle, xvii, 129
cavesson, 5, 13
chambon, 52
changes of direction, 151–155
circle (curves) exercises, 166,
175–176, 190
commandments, training, 3, 149,
185, 187

communication, horse-rider, 2.
  See also aids
conformation, horse's, 1–2,
  130–132, 166
contact, 50, 51–52, 138, 162
counter-canter, 103–106, 182–183.
  See also canter
counter-rein (neck rein), 17, 53–59,
  69, 171
counter-reins of opposition, 17–18,
  90, 172
curb bits, 11–12

D
debourrage, 129
Decarpentry, General, 15, 122–123
direct flexions, 36–37, 41
direction changes, 151–155
direct reins of opposition, 17, 18,
  89–90, 155, 171–172
dressage, definition of, 3, 129–130.
  See also training (dressage)
dressage tests
  canter, 181, 182
  counter-canter, 182
  discouragement, 199
  elegance of horse and, 132
  explanation of, 129
  gear and, 11, 12
  general impressions scores,
    195–197
  halts, 166
  impulsion, 185
  judging in, 195–199
  precision and, 171
  shoulder-in, 191
  size of horse and, 132
  straightness, 186–187
Duplessis, 142

E
École de Cavalerie (La
  Guérinière), 121
elegance, 132
Elémens de Cavalerie (La
  Guérinière), 92

engagement, 25–26, 166
equipment, 5, 11–14, 52
ewe-necked horses, 131, 166
eyesight, 132

F
false canter, 182
Federation Équestre International
  (FEI), 12, 197
fingerplay, 169, 170
flexions. *See also* half-turn on
  forehand (half-pirouette in
  reverse); rein back; suppling
  exercises
  overview, 29–30
  by descent of neck, 43
  direct, 36–37, 41
  at jaw, 30–31, 32–34
  lateral, 31–35, 42–43
  of neck, 30, 31, 35, 43
  neck stretching, 37–39, 44
  relaxation, importance of, 46, 73
flying changes of the leg, 107–109
forehand turns. *See* half-turn on
  forehand (half-pirouette in
  reverse)
forelegs
  formation of, 131
  one-track work and, 189
  pivoting and, 151, 152
  ramener and anatomy of, 160
  reversed half-voltes and, 153
  two-track work and, 189–190
  weight distribution and, 157–158
forward movement
  balance and, 158
  bits and, 139–140
  impulsion *vs.*, 185
  obedience and, 55
  rein back and, 170, 171
  as training commandment, 3, 149,
    185, 187
  training techniques for, 49–50,
    185–186
French School, 121–124
full bridle, 11

G

gaits, 167, 175, 176, 177, 186
gear, 5, 11–14
geldings, 131
Germanic School, 93, 121–124
Grand Prix de Dressage, 152, 197
Guérinière. *See* La Guérinière,
  François Robichone de

H

hacks, 53, 56, 132–133
half-halts, 15
half-pass
  circle, 99–100
  counter-changes of hand in, 100
  exercise techniques for, 97–101,
    192–193
  horse alignment during, 189
  placer for, 75
half-pirouette in reverse. *See* half-
  turn on forehand
half-turn on forehand (half-pirouette
  in reverse)
  aids usage and, 69, 147–148
  leg action in, 140
  in training for half-turn on
    haunches, 163
  training instructions for, 40, 65–66,
    111–112, 151–153
half-turn on haunches, 66, 68–73,
  151, 163–165
half-voltes, 153, 189, 192
halts
  immobility period during, 167, 170
  judging of, 166, 167
  obtaining effective, 49, 165–166
  and slowdowns, 54
  square, 55
hands
  for canter departures, 181
  effectiveness of, 16
  half-turn on forehand and, 69,
    147–148
  halts and, 167
  with leg coordination, 141–142
  operation of, 15–16, 137, 139, 141

ramener and, 159, 162
rein back fingerplay, 169, 170
relaxation of, 16, 139
role in contact, 50–51
slow downs and, 167, 176
in suppling exercises, 176
haunches
  changes of direction and, 151–152
  lateral mobility for pirouettes, 111
  lightness importance, 151
  rein effects on, 17–18, 171
  teaching lateral mobilization of,
    65–66
haunches, half-turn on, 66, 68–73,
  151, 163–165
haunch-in, 95–97
haute école, 23, 111, 129
head carriage, 159. *See also placer;*
  ramener
heel position, 136
hindlegs
  engagement of, 25–26, 166, 175
  half-turn on haunches and, 163, 165
  halts and, 166
  neck stretching and, 51
  one-track work and, 189
  ramener and anatomy of, 160
  reversed half-voltes and, 153
  two-track work and, 189–190
  weight distribution and, 157–158
hindquarters. *See* haunches
horses
  acquaintance with, 132–133
  age for training, 2, 130
  character of, 53, 131, 150
  conformation of, 1–2, 130–132, 166
  ewe-necked, 131, 166
  selection of, 1–2, 130–132
  sensitivity of, 138
  weight distribution of, 157–158
  well-being of, 1, 53, 132, 133

I

immobility, 8, 48, 62, 167, 170
impulsion, 54–55, 137, 185, 189
intermediate rein, 17–18, 90, 172

J

jaw exercises, 30–31, 32–34
judges, 195–199. *See also* dressage
    tests
jumping, 61–63, 107–108, 195, 197

K

keenness, 133

L

La Guérinière, François Robichone
    de, xvii, 92–93, 113, 121–124
lateral flexions, 31–35, 42–43
lateral suppling, 75–81, 175–176
legs, rider's
    canter departures and, 86–87,
        180–181
    during dressage tests, 196
    half-turn on forehand and, 140,
        147, 153
    halts and, 167
    with hand coordination, 141–142
    operation of, 16, 19, 54, 138,
        139–140
    positioning of, 136
    position *vs.* action, 181
    single leg action, 19, 155, 163
    in suppling exercises, 175, 176
    whip association and, 50, 54
Lesage, Colonel, 124
"lesson of the legs," 50
lessons, 8, 62, 133
L'Hotte, General Alexis, 3
Licart, Major, 24
lightness, 151, 152, 160, 186
Loerke, Otto, 124
longitudinal suppling, 81–84,
    176–177
lungelines, 5–6
lunging, 5–9, 54

M

manege work, 131
mares, 131
martingales, standing, 12
methodical procedure, 148

mind, as aid, xx
mise en main, 84
Morris, General, 21
mounting, 47–49, 62
mouth, horse's, 139, 162. *See also* bits

N

neck
    carriage of, 27, 28
    effect of bridle on, in early
        training, 50
    examination in horse selection, 131
    flexions of the, 30, 31, 37, 43
    inflection during counter-
        canter, 183
    orientation of, for selection, 27
    ramener and position of, 160–161
    role in engagement, 25
    stretching of, 27, 37–39, 44, 51–52,
        161–162
neck rein (counter-rein), 17, 57–59,
    69, 171
Newcastle, Duke of. *See* Cavendish,
    William, Duke of Newcastle
nosebands, 5, 11–14

O

obedience, 8, 37, 53, 55, 148–149
one-track work, 189
opening rein, 16–17, 69, 171

P

paces, 52
passage, 115–117
patience, 132
philosophy of dressage, 3, 149,
    185, 187
piaffe, 117–119, 185
pirouettes, 111–114. *See also* half-
    turn on forehand (half-pirouette
    in reverse)
placer
    aids for, 67
    canter, 103
    counter-canter, 103–104
    for counter shoulder-in, 75

definition of, 58
half-pass, 75
shoulder-in, 75
position, rider's, 135–136, 196. *See also* seat
punishments, 6, 148–149

Q
Questions Equestres (L'Hotte), 3

R
ramener, 24, 27–28, 158–162
Rau, Dr., 122
rein back
    fingerplay for, 169, 170
    flexions for, 41, 46
    in longitudinal suppling, 81–83
    problems encountered, 169
    training techniques for, 170–171
reins. *See also* rein back
    combing (stroking) the, 52, 162
    neck stretching and, 37–39, 51–52, 162
    positioning of, 137
    rigid, 55–56
    running, 12
reins effects, five, 16–18, 57–59, 89–90, 155, 171–174
relaxation, 46, 73. *See also* flexions
resistance, 106, 142, 163, 176
resisting operations, 16, 137–138
reversed half-voltes, 153–154, 189
rewards, 8, 37, 53, 148–149
rising trot, 62, 162, 179

S
saddle position, 135–136, 196
Saumur (Cavalry School), 122, 124, 137
Saunier, Gaspar de, 142
School of Versailles, 122
seat, 136, 140–141, 181–182
shoulder-in, 90–95, 104–105, 189, 190–192
show competitions, 195, 197. See *also* dressage tests

sickle hocks, 131–132
size of horse, 132
slow downs, 54, 167, 176, 181
snaffles, 11, 12, 13. *See also* bridles
Spanische Hofreitschule, 122
speed-ups, 176–177, 181
spurs, 49, 66–67, 137, 181, 185
standing martingales, 12
steadiness, rider's, 141
straightness
    during canter, 103, 105, 181
    during counter-canter, 105
    suppling exercises for, 175, 176
    as training commandment, 186–187
stride, 83–84
strike-offs, 179, 180
submission, first act of, 48
suppleness, rider's, 136, 141
suppling exercises. *See also* flexions
    lateral, 75–81, 175–176
    longitudinal, 81–84, 176–177

T
tail, 131
tests. *See* dressage tests
toe position, 136
tongues, lolling, 130
training (dressage)
    overview, 2–3
    commandments of, 3, 149, 185, 187
    equestrian term for, 3, 129–130
    lessons, 8, 62, 133
    principles of, xix–xx
    "the training period," 147
trotting, 6, 169, 176–177, 179, 196
turns, 66, 68–73, 151, 163–165. *See also* half-turn on forehand (half-pirouette in reverse)
two-track work, 89–101, 189–193

V
Versailles, School of, 122
vetting, 1, 132
voice, as aid, 6, 54, 179, 180
von Holzing, General, 122–123

W

weight distribution
  as aid, 19–20
  effect on the horse, 23–28,
    50, 136, 140–141,
    181–182
  experiments in, 21–23,
    157–158
  selection of horse and, 131

whips
  leg association with, 50, 54
  lunging, 5, 8
  riding, 29, 49, 137, 185

Y

yielding operations, 15, 16, 137–138,
  176
Y-mouth snaffles, 11